The
UNITED STATES

Part 2

Industrialization to the Present

Diane Hart

Consultants

David Scofield Wilson, Ph.D.
Associate Professor,
American Studies Program
University of California, Davis
Davis, California

Sherman Lewis, Ph.D.
Professor of Political Science
California State University
Hayward, California

Age of
Industry

World War I

World War II

A World Power

Great Depression

Age of
Technology

Janus Books

Janus Books

a division of
Janus Book Publishers, Inc.

2501 Industrial Parkway West
Hayward, CA 94545
(415) 887-7070

Janus Social Studies Books

International Standard Book Number
0-88102-058-3

8 9 0 1 2 3 4 5 6 D — P 0 9 8 7 6 5 4 3 2

Project Editor: Winifred Ho Roderman
Editor: Dennis Binkley
Assistant Editors: Valle Brokes, Joan Felder
Artist: Margaret Sanfilippo
Maps: C. Buck Reynolds
Cover photos: R. Krubner/H. Armstrong Roberts
Designer: E. Carol Gee

Production Manager: E. Carol Gee
Manufacturing Administrator: Elizabeth Tong
Composition Administrator: Arlene Hardwick
Typographer: Letter Perfect Typography
Printer: WCP, Inc.

Acknowledgments: We would like to thank the
following people for their time and generosity:
Bryan Headley, Photo Researcher; Daniel K.
Inouye, United States Senator, Hawaii;
Kathleen Manning, Prints Old and Rare,
San Francisco; Photo Lab Staff, Hoover Dam;
Photo Library, Dept. of Public Information, The
United Nations; Roseanne Bell, NASA-Ames
Research Center; Lee Amazonis, Archivist,
Pacific Film Archive, University of California,
Berkeley; Olan Blue, Assistant to the Curator,
Pictorial Collection, Bancroft Library,
University of California, Berkeley; The
Des Moines *Register*; John Carter, Photo
Archives, The Nebraska Historical Society;
Phil Mooney, Archivist, The Coca-Cola Company,
Christine Lindmark, Researcher.

This book is brought to you by: Shipping
Carl Gaines, M.E. Knox, Jose Pulido, Ray
Rubio, Jackie Williams/**Order Processing** Sue
Bueno, Mechelle Cochran, Sandy Hedrick,
Joanne Helms, Linda Jang, Hallie Mann,
Maureen Plevin, Michele Wilson/**Accounting**
Pam Eddy, Irma Nieves, Helen Tong, Judy Tong/
Marketing Jane Brundage, Alice Moreno, Roger
Olsen, Sylvia Jordan/**Production** Carol Gee,
Arlene Hardwick, Carolyn Reynolds, Elizabeth
Tong/**Editorial** Dennis Binkley, Valle Brokes,
Joan Felder, Irma Mendonca, Helen Munch,
Winifred Roderman, Joan Wolfgang/
Administration Nicholas J. Randall,
Robert Tong

Industrialization to the Present

Contents

Age of Industry

1865–1900   1900   World War I   1929–1939   World War II   1945–
                              1914–1918   1939–1945

            A World Power   Great Depression   Age of Technology

Introduction

The year 1876 was the nation's *centennial year.* Just a century before, in 1776, Americans had declared their independence and begun a new nation, the United States of America.

In 1776, the United States was a small nation of less than three million Americans. It had just 13 states, all on the eastern shore of the continent. By 1876, the United States had grown to a nation of 46 million Americans. It stretched across the continent, from sea to shining sea. It had 38 states, vast frontier territories in its West, and island territories in the Pacific.

During the centennial year, every town, village, and city held a celebration. But the biggest was in Philadelphia, the city where the Declaration of Independence had been signed. Millions of Americans came to Philadelphia to visit the *Centennial Exposition.* That was a huge fair with hundreds of displays.

Visitors crowded around displays showing the most modern machines and inventions. Fairgoers admired the new sewing machines, the new soda fountains, and the huge Corliss steam engine. It was over 20 feet high and provided all the electric power for the fair.

Industrialization to the Present

Americans at the Exposition were proud of America's new machines and inventions. They were proud of the way the country had changed and grown during its first hundred years. But they would have been amazed if they could have seen the machines and inventions that would be made in the next 100 years. And they would have found it hard to believe the changes to come.

In the next several weeks, you will be reading Part 2 of a history of the United States. It is the story of America's second 100 years. You will learn how America became an industrial nation, how it became the most powerful nation in the world, and how it fought to bring democracy to other countries. You will learn how Americans of all races work for equal rights. And you will learn about challenges that face Americans today.

As you read about America's second hundred years, you will find it easier to understand events that are happening today. You'll better understand the ideas that your nation is based on. And you'll be better able to help meet the challenges faced by Americans in the world today.

American history is not over. It is still being made. And you are part of it.

unit 6 Building an Industrial Nation

Menlo Park, New Jersey — October 21, 1879

Inside a dark workshop, Thomas Edison and his workers gather around his latest invention—an electric lamp. "Are we ready to test it?" asks Edison.

For over a year, he has been trying to use electricity to make a lamp. His idea is to put a thin *filament* (thread) inside a glass bulb and run electricity through it. The electricity should heat the filament until it glows and gives off light.

So far, Edison has not been able to make a lamp work. Each time he runs electricity through a filament, it melts. Will this one melt too?

Edison turns on the electricity—and the lamp glows. Hours pass. Days pass. The lamp finally dims and goes out. It has burned for 45 hours!

Edison boasts: "If the lamp can burn for 45 hours, I can make it burn for 100!"

Edison has created an electric lamp. But he realizes that people cannot use his invention unless they have electricity. Edison decides to build an electric power system that can bring electricity to workplaces and homes in New York City.

On September 4, 1882, the new electric power system is ready. The city glows with electric light. A new industry is born. And the world enters the electric age.

In Our Time

During the late 1800s, the United States changed rapidly from a nation of farms to a nation of factories. New inventions changed the ways people worked and lived. Small towns grew into large cities.

Inventions are still being created in the United States today. What inventions are changing the way we live? How are they changing our lives?

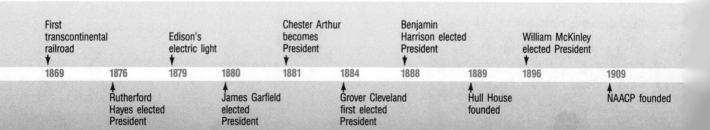

First transcontinental railroad		Edison's electric light		Chester Arthur becomes President		Benjamin Harrison elected President		William McKinley elected President	
1869	1876	1879	1880	1881	1884	1888	1889	1896	1909
	Rutherford Hayes elected President		James Garfield elected President		Grover Cleveland first elected President		Hull House founded		NAACP founded

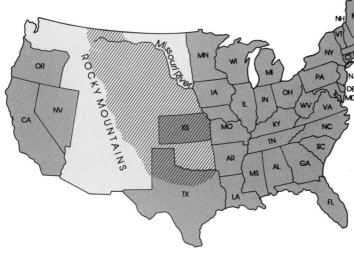

THE UNITED STATES IN 1865

- States admitted to the Union
- Great Plains
- U.S. territory

Chapter 16 Settling the West

In 1865, most of the West—the land that stretched westward from the Missouri River to the Pacific Ocean—was United States territory. Much of the West was made up of flat, grassy land called the Great Plains. It stretched from Texas to Canada. Settlers crossed the Great Plains to get to California, Nevada, and Oregon. They traveled by wagon or stagecoach.

By 1900, just 35 years later, almost all of the West had become new western states. The rapid settlement of the West came about because of the building of railroads. Trains carried thousands of settlers westward.

For the settlers, moving to the West meant beginning a new life. For the Indian peoples of the West, it meant the end of their way of life.

- How did railroads help settle the West?
- Why were railroads important to western towns?
- What happened to Indians in the West when the settlers came?

Key Words   You will be using these words in this chapter. Look them up in the glossary at the back of Part 2.

boom   **invasion**
homesteader   **transcontinental**

Railroads Open the West

Congress wanted a rail line that would cross the continent. To build that *transcontinental* rail line, railroad tracks would have to be laid thousands of miles across the West. The Union Pacific and the Central Pacific railroad companies were chosen to do the job.

The Union Pacific Railroad started from Omaha, Nebraska. Most of its workers were Irish immigrants. They laid tracks across the flat Plains and across the rugged Rocky Mountains.

The Central Pacific started work at the other end of the line, in Sacramento, California. Its workers were mostly Chinese immigrants. They cut a route through the Sierra Nevada and across the hot deserts of Nevada.

On May 10, 1869, the tracks of the two railroads came together at Promontory, Utah. For the first time, people could travel by train from the Atlantic to the Pacific Ocean.

Other railroad lines were soon built. By 1893, five transcontinental railroad lines were carrying people to the unsettled areas in the West.

Looking Back
1. What is a transcontinental railroad?
2. Who were the immigrant workers who laid the tracks?
3. How do people travel across the country today?

Ranchers and Homesteaders

As soon as railroads connected the West and the East, the West began to change. Railroads helped bring about a *cattle boom*—a time when the cattle business grew very rapidly.

At the end of the Civil War, cattle sold for about $4 a head in Texas. But cattle sold for about $40 a head in large eastern cities. In 1867, a cattle dealer named **J.G. McCoy** figured out a way to get Texas cattle to the East.

The First Long Cattle Drive

McCoy hired cowboys to round up a large herd of Texas cattle. Cowboys on horses then kept the cattle moving, driving them north for a thousand miles. The *cattle drive* ended at Abilene, Kansas. There, the cattle were loaded on trains and shipped east. McCoy made a lot of money.

Other ranchers followed McCoy's example. They sent cowboys on huge cattle drives to western railroad towns. Soon, selling Texas cattle became an important business. Ranchers began looking for places to raise more cattle.

Cattle Ranches on the Open Range

On the Plains north of Texas, millions of acres of unfenced grassland belonged to the federal government. That land was called the *open range*, and anyone could graze cattle on it. Cattle ranching spread across the open range from Texas to Canada. Some ranchers owned thousands of cattle. Great herds of their cattle grazed for miles on the open range.

But the open range did not last long. The railroads brought **homesteaders** to the Plains. The homesteaders built homes on the open range. They turned the grazing land into farms and put up fences to keep the cattle out. By 1890, the open range was gone, and the cattle boom was over.

Artist Hugo Nahl, who lived from 1833 to 1889, painted this picture. It shows cowboys in California catching wild horses.

The Oakland Museum Kahn Collection

Homesteaders Settle on the Plains

When easterners first crossed the Great Plains, they thought the Plains could not be settled or farmed. The climate seemed too dry for crops. There were very few trees for lumber and fuel. And the land was covered with thick *sod*—soil held together by tough grass roots. The sod was difficult to dig or plow.

But new inventions made it possible for people to homestead on the Plains. One of the inventions was the steel plow. It cut easily through the sod. Another invention was barbed wire. Farmers used the wire in place of wooden fences. They used it to keep cattle and other livestock from destroying their crops.

Farmers dug wells and found water deep underground. They learned to raise crops that grew in the dry climate.

Today, wheat, corn, soybeans, and other important crops grow on the Great Plains. That region has become the nation's ''breadbasket.''

Looking Back

1. How did railroads help the cattle boom?
2. What ended the cattle boom?
3. What made it possible for homesteaders to farm the Plains?
4. Why are the Great Plains called the nation's ''breadbasket''?

Solomon D. Butcher Collection Nebraska State Historical Society

This photograph shows the Shores family outside their sod house. They were homesteaders in Custer County, Nebraska, 1887.

Settlers Follow the Railroads

Everywhere railroads went, new towns grew up beside the tracks. DeSmet, South Dakota, was one of those towns.

Laura Ingalls Wilder was a teenager in DeSmet. She wrote many books about her childhood. They tell us what life was like on the Plains. (One of Mrs. Wilder's books, *Little House on the Prairie*, was made into a TV program in the 1970s.)

DeSmet, South Dakota

In 1880, a railroad was being built across South Dakota. Laura Ingalls Wilder described the beginnings of DeSmet.

''Suddenly,'' she wrote, ''there on the brown prairie where nothing had been before, was the town.'' In just two weeks, the main street was lined with buildings. Before long, DeSmet had a school, a church, stores, and a newspaper.

Trains were important to DeSmet and other western towns. Trains brought lumber for houses. They hauled coal. They brought the food and goods that stores sold. And they carried the farmers' crops and livestock back to eastern cities.

A Hard Winter Cuts Off DeSmet

In the winter of 1881, terrible storms swept across the Plains and over DeSmet. The railroad tracks were buried under 40 feet of snow. DeSmet was cut off from the world.

Laura Ingalls Wilder wrote that by February, the town was out of coal. People burned what they could to keep from freezing.

In March, the stores in DeSmet ran out of food. For the next two months, the Ingalls family had nothing to eat except wheat seeds.

Finally, the snows melted enough to let a train through. On May 10, a train reached DeSmet. The hungry people there found it was loaded with farm machinery, not food. But the next day, another train arrived—this time with food and Christmas presents. The people of DeSmet celebrated Christmas in May.

DeSmet continued to grow. Sidewalks took the place of dirt paths. A roller skating rink opened. A soda fountain was built in the drug store. In time, DeSmet became a busy modern town.

Hundreds of towns throughout the West grew like DeSmet. They all began as small settlements next to the railroad tracks.

Looking Back

1. Why did western towns grow up next to railroads?
2. Why was winter a dangerous time for towns along the railroad?
3. Today, towns grow up along highways instead of railroads. Why do you think that is so?

This U.S. postage stamp honors Chief Joseph and the Nez Perce Indians. In 1877, they fought the U.S. Cavalry to keep from being sent to a reservation.

The Plains Indians

Many different Indian peoples lived on the Great Plains. They were buffalo hunters. They lived by following the vast herds of buffalo that roamed across the Plains.

The Indians followed the herds from place to place. They depended on the herds for almost everything. Their main food was buffalo meat. They made tools out of buffalo bones. They made clothes, tents, and blankets from buffalo skins.

Plains Indians Fight for Their Lands

In 1859, gold was found in Colorado. Thousands of miners and settlers rushed across the Plains. Many took over Indian lands.

Some of the Plains Indians went to war against the newcomers. They attacked the settlers, killing hundreds of them. The United States Army took over the job of protecting the settlers. Army Indian fighters killed large numbers of the Plains Indians.

Indians Are Put on Reservations

In 1868, the United States government made treaties with leaders of the largest group of Plains Indians. According to the treaties, the Indians would stay on large reservations. Some Indians agreed to move to the reservations. But many refused. They did not want to give up their way of life.

But that way of life was coming to an end for the Plains Indians. Buffalo herds were disappearing. White hunters were slaughtering buffalo by the millions. Without the buffalo, the Plains Indians could no longer live as they had.

Indian Wars on the Plains

In the southern part of the Plains, the Apache, the Cheyenne, the Arapaho, and the Comanche fought to keep their way of life. They fought battles in Colorado, New Mexico, Kansas, and Texas. Farther north, in Montana and the Dakotas, the Sioux fought to keep their territory.

The Sioux owned a huge territory that included the Black Hills of South Dakota. The Black Hills were their hunting grounds. In 1868, the federal government signed a treaty with the Sioux. The treaty promised the Sioux that the land would always belong to them.

In the 1870s, the government broke the treaty. Gold was found in the Black Hills. An *invasion* of gold seekers filled the territory. The Sioux went to war against the invaders.

In 1876, Sioux warriors fought General **George Custer** and an army of 264 troops at Little Big Horn River, in Montana. General Custer and all his troops were killed.

Although the Sioux won the battle at Little Big Horn, they could not hold out against the United States Army. A few months later, the Sioux surrendered. By 1900, the Indian wars were over.

Looking Back

1. How did the Plains Indians live before settlers came?
2. Why did the Plains Indians go to war against settlers in 1859?
3. Why did many Indians refuse to live on reservations?
4. How did the government break its promises to the Sioux?

Life on the Reservations

Whenever settlers moved onto Indian lands in the West, conflict followed. The government tried to end those conflicts by forcing Indians to live on reservations.

The Government Makes Promises

The government made many promises to Indians who moved to reservations. It promised to give them food and supplies. It promised to teach the Indians how to farm so they could live off their lands. And it promised that the lands of the reservations would belong forever to the Indians; the government would make sure no one took away those lands.

Some Indians accepted reservation life. But many hated it. They were hunters.

Government Promises Are Broken

Promises that the government made to provide food and protect the reservations were soon broken. Food did not arrive, or it came spoiled. Railroad crews laid tracks across reservations. Miners looked for gold on Indian lands. Outsiders came onto the reservations and cut down trees.

Some Indians wanted to go back to a life of hunting. But when they left the reservations, they were hunted down by army Indian fighters. Many of those Indians chose to fight the army troops rather than return to the reservations.

The Dawes Act Divides Indian Lands

By 1886, almost all the Indian peoples in the United States had been forced to move to reservations. Each reservation was the property of an Indian people. Then in 1887, Congress passed the **Dawes Act**. The Act broke up the reservations into small units of 40 to 160 acres. Those units were given to individual Indians. Land that was left over was sold to Whites.

The money that the government made by selling Indian lands was supposed to be used to teach the Indians how to farm. Government officials wanted the Indians to settle and stay on reservation lands and not move freely, as they had before.

But most Indians wanted to keep their Indian way of life. They did not like farming on the reservations. Besides, much of the reservation land was too poor to be farmed. So, many Indians sold their lands to Whites. Once their money was gone, those Indians had nothing to live on.

The Ghost Dance

In 1890, a new religion spread among the Sioux. The religion was called the **Ghost Dance**, and it was started by an Indian named Wovoka. Wovoka believed that the old Indian way of life would return. He said that the Whites would disappear, and the great herds of buffalo would come back.

Army leaders were afraid that the religion would stir up the Sioux and cause another uprising. They sent troops to a Sioux reservation in South Dakota.

A band of Indians escaped from the reservation and joined another group on the Cheyenne River. But those Indians were caught by army troops. They were taken to an army camp near Wounded Knee Creek, in South Dakota. Somehow a battle started. When it was over, more than 200 Indian men, women, and children were dead.

Looking Back

1. What did the government promise Indians who lived on reservations?
2. How did the government break its promises?
3. What did the Dawes Act do?
4. Why did army leaders fear the Ghost Dance religion?

Chapter 16

Review

Facts First

Complete each sentence by choosing the correct ending.

1. The first transcontinental railroad
   a. carried goods from New York to Maine.
   b. carried settlers west.
   c. helped the Union win the Civil War.
2. Workers who built the railroads were mainly
   a. cowboys.
   b. homesteaders.
   c. Irish and Chinese immigrants.
3. Railroads helped the cattle boom by
   a. bringing farmers to the Great Plains.
   b. bringing barbed wire west.
   c. carrying cattle to eastern markets.
4. The cattle boom ended when
   a. farmers fenced off the open range.
   b. easterners stopped buying beef.
   c. railroads were built.
5. The movement of settlers west led to
   a. another civil war.
   b. conflict with western Indians.
   c. Indians moving back east.
6. Most Plains Indians lived by
   a. farming.
   b. fishing.
   c. hunting.
7. The government forced western Indians to
   a. live on reservations.
   b. follow the Ghost Dance religion.
   c. move back east.
8. For Indians, moving to a reservation
   a. was the start of a better life.
   b. meant the end of their way of life.
   c. was a chance to hunt buffalo again.

Word Check

Write the meaning of each of these words. Then use each word in a sentence.

boom	**invasion**
homesteader	**transcontinental**

Skill Builder

Trace the routes of these early transcontinental railroad lines on a map (or draw them on an outline map).

1. *The Northern Pacific Line*
   Start at Duluth, Minnesota. Go west across North Dakota, Montana, and Idaho to Seattle, Washington.
2. *The Southern Pacific Line*
   Start at New Orleans, Louisiana. Go west across Texas, New Mexico, and Arizona to Los Angeles, California.

Chapter 16 Notes

Read over the chapter. Find answers to these questions:

1. How did railroads help the West become settled?
2. How did railroads help start a cattle boom?
3. How did Plains farmers help end the cattle boom?
4. How did the settling of the West affect the Plains Indians?

Be a Historian

The words below developed during the time of the great cattle herds. Many of the words are still used today. Find out what they all mean.

bunkhouse	Levi's
bronco	rustler
chuckwagon	six-shooter
lariat	tenderfoot

Bonus

If you know a Native American, interview that person. Ask that person to tell you about the history of Native Americans in the 1800s. If *you* are a Native American, ask one of your parents or grandparents about that time.

Chapter 17 The Growth of Industry

Historical Pictures Service, Chicago

One of the first big businesses in America was in oil. This photograph, made in 1865, shows an oil field in Pioneer Run, Pennsylvania.

After the Civil War, inventors developed many inventions that completely changed how Americans lived, worked, and traveled. Those inventions helped create many new kinds of businesses.

Americans also began to develop new ideas about how to start and run businesses. Because of those new ideas, many small businesses rapidly grew and spread. Those businesses quickly became huge industries that needed thousands of workers. Soon, more Americans would be working on jobs in industries than on farms.

- What important inventions were developed between 1850 and 1900?
- What industries developed after the Civil War?
- How did American life change after the Civil War?

Key Words   You will be using these words in this chapter. Look them up in the glossary at the back of Part 2.

competition	**manufacture**
industry	**product**

New Inventions Change America

Probably the greatest inventor of his time was **Thomas Alva Edison**. Between 1869 and 1931, the year of his death, he created hundreds of inventions. Every time you turn on a light, listen to a phonograph, or watch a movie, you are using one of Edison's inventions.

In 1879, Edison invented a lamp that turned electrical energy into light. Then he built electric power plants to bring electricity for the lamp to homes and businesses.

Americans soon found other uses for the electricity. They used it to run machines. People all across the nation began using electric machines in homes, mills, factories, and business offices.

The Typewriter and the Telephone

New inventions were also improving the ways people could communicate. Two were the typewriter and the telephone.

The typewriter was invented in 1867 by Christopher L. Sholes, Carlos Glidden, and Samuel W. Soule. In the 1870s, people began using the typewriter in business and government offices.

In 1876, **Alexander Graham Bell** invented the *telephone*. It carried speech over an electric wire. A year later, the Bell Telephone Company was started. Soon, people would be able to talk to each other across a town or across a continent.

Other Inventions

Some other inventions that were developed between 1850 and 1900 were the elevator, the cash register, dynamite, the diesel engine, the zipper, the radio, and the x-ray machine. How do you think each changed American life?

AP/Wide World Photos

Library of Congress   Library of Congress

Left: This photograph shows the historic first flight of the Wright brothers on December 17, 1903. *Middle*: By the 1890s, about 4 million Americans were riding bicycles. The bikes in this photograph are unusual in that the small wheel is in front. *Right*: In the 1890s, early cars were called "horseless carriages" because they still looked like the carriages that were pulled by horses.

Inventions in Transportation

By the end of the 1800s, railroad lines were all over the country. Using those railroad lines, Americans could travel from one part of the country to another. But Americans also wanted to get around the towns and cities they lived in. They began using a European invention, the bicycle. By 1900, ten million bicycles were being used in the United States.

Automobiles Come to America

In the 1890s, another European invention came to America—the automobile. It was faster than the bicycle and could carry more people. At first, only the rich had automobiles. Still, by 1900, more than 8000 automobiles were being used in the nation.

Pioneers in Powered Flight

For years, inventors in Europe and the United States had been experimenting with machines that could fly. During the late 1800s, French inventors developed *airships* that were made from huge balloons filled with a gas. Those airships had engines and propellors. At the same time, inventors in France, England, and the United States were experimenting with

airplanes—flying machines that were powered by steam or gasoline engines. So far, no one had been successful in keeping an airplane up in the air.

The First Successful Airplane Flight

Orville Wright and **Wilbur Wright** were American brothers who owned a bicycle repair shop. They became interested in airplanes. In 1899, they began to build and experiment with airplanes that had gasoline engines. On December 17, 1903, Orville Wright flew one of those airplanes at Kitty Hawk, North Carolina. The airplane was in the air for 12 seconds. It was the Wrights' first successful flight. On later flights, they flew the airplane for longer and longer periods of time.

The Wright brothers showed that airplanes could travel in the air. They and other inventors worked to develop airplanes that could make longer flights. In a few years, airplanes would become an important form of transportation for the world.

Looking Back

1. What inventions helped Americans get around in cities and towns?
2. How did the Wright brothers help to change the way people traveled?

Organizing Big Businesses

Before the Civil War, most businesses were small. They hired only a few workers. The businesses were usually started by one person or a few people who were partners. Those people put together the money that was needed to start the business. They shared the *profit* made by the business. (A profit is the money a business has left after it pays all its expenses.)

But that way of starting didn't work for businesses such as railroads. Those businesses cost *millions* of dollars to start. That was more money than one person or a few partners could raise. So, people began to organize those businesses in a new way. They formed **corporations**. Most new businesses after the Civil War began as corporations.

Corporations: Businesses with Many Owners

A corporation is a business that is owned by many people. It is started by someone who has the idea for the business. That person then sells shares of the business to other people. The shares are called *stock*. The more shares of stock the person sells, the more money he or she can raise. That money is used to build the business.

The people who buy shares in the business are called *stockholders*. Together, stockholders own the corporation. Those who own the most shares of stock own most of the business. When the corporation makes a profit, that money is divided among the stockholders. Stockholders with more stock get more of the profit.

When a corporation does well, the price of a share goes up. (The price falls when business is bad.) Stockholders can sell their stock. They make money when they sell their stock for more money than they paid to buy it.

Carnegie Steel Corporation

One of the largest corporations formed after the Civil War was the Carnegie Steel Company. It was organized by **Andrew Carnegie** in 1873. Carnegie was an immigrant from Scotland.

When Carnegie organized the corporation, steel was expensive to **manufacture**, so its price was high. Carnegie used a new method of making steel that was fast and cheap. He then sold his steel at prices most businesses could afford. Manufacturers in many businesses began using steel. The steel business became an important **industry** for the nation.

One of the First Big Businesses

Carnegie's first steel mill was built near Pittsburgh, Pennsylvania. At first, Carnegie bought the iron ore needed to make steel from mining companies in Minnesota. He paid shipping and railroad companies to send the ore to his mill. Then Carnegie bought his own Minnesota iron mines. He bought his own ships and railroads to carry the ore. He took control of every step in the production of steel.

Such methods allowed Carnegie to keep his prices low and still make a profit. With that profit, he bought smaller steel companies. By 1900, the Carnegie Steel Company was the nation's largest steelmaker—and one of the nation's first big businesses. The corporation produced one-fourth of all the nation's steel. In 1901, Carnegie sold his stock in the corporation. He made $250 million from the sale.

Looking Back
1. Why did people begin to form corporations?
2. How did corporations raise money to build businesses?
3. How did Andrew Carnegie help the steel industry grow?

Controlling Competition

Many of the businesses that sprang up after the Civil War made the same *products*. To get customers to buy their products, companies went into *competition* with each other. They improved their products. They also lowered their prices.

Competition Leads to Price Wars

Competition was good for customers. They had many well-made products to choose from. And they could buy things cheaply.

But competition often led to **price wars** that were bad for some companies. In those price wars, each company tried to make its products or services the cheapest by constantly cutting prices. Sometimes, prices dropped far below the cost of running the company. Only the strongest companies could survive a long price war. The weak ones ran out of money and went out of business.

The Standard Oil Trust

In 1859, many people were in the *oil refinery* business. An oil refinery is a factory that makes products, such as kerosene, from oil. Too many refineries produced too much kerosene. A price war broke out, and everyone lost money.

One of the people who owned a refinery was a businessman named **John D. Rockefeller**. Rockefeller thought such competition was wasteful. He decided that it made more sense for one business to control all the nation's refineries. He formed the Standard Oil Company in 1870. Standard Oil then tried to buy competing refineries or to drive them out of business.

In 1882, Rockefeller organized the Standard Oil *Trust*. The trust was another new way to organize a business: It let people who owned stock in one company trade it for stock in another company.

Many refinery owners traded their stock for Standard Oil stock in that way. Standard Oil became the owner of almost all the refineries in the United States.

The Rise of Monopolies

Standard Oil soon had a **monopoly** of the oil business. When a company has a monopoly, it has practically no competition. It is nearly the only company that makes and sells certain products.

Many companies followed the example of Standard Oil. They also formed trusts and took control of competing companies. Soon, trusts controlled the manufacture of whiskey, lead, sugar, and other important products.

Railroads Agree to Control Competition

Railroads also wanted to control competition. Competition was fierce in the railroad industry, and price wars went on all the time. Many railroad companies failed or were in danger of failing.

To solve their problems, managers of different railroad companies agreed to end the price wars. They agreed that only certain companies would do business in certain areas. And they agreed to charge the same rates. In that way, each company could make money.

The end of competition meant good business for all the railroad companies. But it meant higher prices for customers. Because they had no competition, the companies could raise their prices as high as they pleased.

Looking Back
1. Why is competition among businesses good for customers?
2. How did John D. Rockefeller end competition in the oil business?
3. What happens when a company has a monopoly?
4. Why are monopolies bad for customers?

Controlling Big Business

Big businesses grew rapidly after the Civil War under a system of **free enterprise**. In a free enterprise system, the government has very little to do with the nation's businesses. People can go into any business they wish. They can decide what to produce, how much to produce, and what prices to charge. They can compete in any way they choose. For example, if they wish to change their prices, they can do so at any time.

Americans believed in the free enterprise system. They believed people should be left alone to run their businesses. But by the 1880s, some people were worried about the power of big businesses.

Unfair Business Competition

Big companies at that time used many unfair business practices to take business away from their competitors. They made secret deals with transportation companies to ship their products at special rates. They hired spies. They bribed lawmakers to pass laws that helped one company over another.

Monopolies End Competition

Many Americans also began to worry about monopolies. As you read, many companies ended competition in their business by forming trusts. Those trusts became monopolies.

People began to say that monopolies were not good for free enterprise. Monopolies drove too many small companies out of business. Without competition, there was nothing to keep the big businesses from raising their prices. There was also no reason for the businesses to improve their products or services.

The Government Tries to Regulate Business

Americans began to demand that Congress do something to *regulate*, or control, the giant corporations.

This political cartoon was drawn in 1889. The artist shows how huge monopolies have grown. At right is little Uncle Sam.

Congress looked first at the railroads. In 1887, it passed a law that set up the **Interstate Commerce Commission (ICC)**. A commission is a group of people chosen to do a job. The Interstate Commerce Commission's job was to make sure that railroad rates were fair.

Then Congress attacked the trusts. In 1890, it passed a law called the **Sherman Antitrust Act**. The purpose of the law was to break up monopolies into smaller businesses. Those smaller businesses would have to compete with each other.

The railroads and trusts fought the new laws in the federal courts. The courts sided with the businesses. Judges ruled that people and businesses should be free to do as they wanted. The judges said that was the idea of the free enterprise system.

Even so, those two laws were important. For the first time, Congress had said that the government should regulate business for the good of the people. In the future, government control would increase.

Looking Back

1. How does the free enterprise system work?
2. How did some big businesses compete unfairly?
3. How did Congress try to regulate big business?

New City Skylines

America's new industries caused cities to grow rapidly. Most businesses were started in cities, where they could find workers and transportation systems. When the businesses grew, they created many jobs. Those jobs brought more people into the cities.

Chicago: Big City of the Midwest

The city that grew most rapidly after the Civil War was Chicago. In 1830, Chicago was a village of log huts. Just 40 years later, it had become a city of 300,000 people. It had also become the nation's transportation and industrial center.

Chicago grew rapidly because of railroads. By 1856, ten main railroad lines went through the city. Almost 100 trains came and went every day. They could move people and goods to other cities in all parts of the country.

Cattle ranchers, farmers, and lumber companies in the West shipped their products to the East through Chicago. Factories in the East shipped goods to the West through Chicago. By 1870, Chicago was the center for the livestock, meat-packing, grain, farm machinery, and lumber industries.

The excellent transportation network caused many other industries to develop in Chicago. One of the new businesses was Montgomery Ward and Company. It was a mail-order business that sold goods by advertising them in a catalog. It shipped goods to customers all over the nation.

In 1871, a fire broke out that destroyed most of the city. Over the next few years, Chicago was quickly rebuilt. By 1890, over a million people were living in Chicago. It was the second largest city in the United States.

Buildings Scrape the Sky

As the nation's cities grew, they became more and more crowded. People who moved to the cities wanted to live and work right in the center of those cities.

The cities needed new buildings for businesses and homes. But the cities were running out of space. Builders began to talk of building upward. They wanted to build very tall buildings that could hold hundreds of people.

Until the 1880s, most large buildings were made of bricks. Very few buildings were as much as five stories high. Tall buildings had to have very thick lower walls that could support the weight of the upper stories. The taller the buildings, the thicker the walls had to be.

A New Kind of Building

The new iron and steel industries gave builders a way to make buildings that could be unbelievably tall. Builders first made a metal frame for the building. Then they covered the frame with thin walls of bricks or concrete. Those buildings were so tall that they were called *skyscrapers*.

The first skyscraper was built in Chicago, after the great fire. By 1900, skyscrapers were all over Chicago and New York City. Thousands of people worked and lived in the tall buildings.

Looking Back

1. How did new industries help cities grow?
2. Why did Chicago become the nation's industrial center?
3. Why were skyscrapers built in cities?
4. What are the largest businesses and industries in your town or city?

Chapter 17

Review

Facts First

Use words below to complete each sentence.

Andrew Carnegie	**free enterprise**
Antitrust Act	**industry**
automobile	**skyscrapers**
competition	**stockholders**
electric light	**trusts**

1. Edison's _____ led to the creation of the electric power industry.
2. _____ built the nation's largest steel corporation.
3. The _____ gave people new freedom to travel.
4. People who buy shares of a company are _____.
5. The _____ system left people free to run their businesses as they pleased.
6. The public liked _____ among businesses because it usually kept prices low.
7. Some business people tried to reduce competition by forming _____.
8. Congress passed the Sherman _____ to try to break up monopolies.
9. The growth of _____ brought people to cities seeking jobs.
10. More people could live and work in the city centers after _____ were built.

Word Check

Write the meaning of each of these words. Then use each word in a sentence.

competition	**manufacture**
industry	**product**

Skill Builder

Make an "Invention Timeline" that shows each invention below. Begin with the year 1852. End with the year 1903.

electric light (1879)	typewriter (1867)
phonograph (1877)	automobile (1886)
passenger elevator (1852)	airplane (1903)
	skyscraper (1884)
	telephone (1876)

Chapter 17 Notes

Read over the chapter. Find answers to these questions:

1. What were three important inventions of the late 1800s? How did each change the way people lived?
2. What are stockholders? How can they make money from their stock?
3. How was competition good for customers but harmful for some businesses?
4. Why did people think monopolies were not good for the free enterprise system?
5. What two actions did Congress take to try to regulate big business?

Be a Historian

Find out how important electric power is to you. Go through your house and garage. List everything that uses electricity. List everything that plugs into an outlet or uses batteries.

Bonus

In the 1880s, government began to try to regulate businesses. Today, the government still wants to make sure businesses are responsible and treat customers fairly. Call the Food and Drug Administration or the Consumer Product Safety Commission in your city or town. Find out what they do to help customers.

Chapter 18   **The Struggle for a Better Life**

Library of Congress

This engraving is from a news magazine. It shows immigrants arriving in New York in the late 1890s.

In the 1800s, millions of immigrants came to the United States. They hoped to find a better life in the new land. Some of them settled in the West. But most of them came to the cities.

Americans from farms and villages also came to the cities, looking for jobs and a better life. The rapid growth of cities and industries brought new problems. Americans began to work to correct those problems.

- How did most new immigrants live and work in America?
- What problems developed for people in the cities?
- How did reformers work to improve the lives of Americans?

Key Words   You will be using these words in this chapter. Look them up in the glossary at the back of Part 2.

ethnic   segregate
labor union   strike

A Nation of Immigrants

From the very beginning, the United States has been a nation of immigrants. Since the founding of the first colonies, people have left their homelands to immigrate to America. They come from all over the world, from many different *ethnic* backgrounds.

Immigrants Search for a Better Life

In the 1800s, life was not easy in Europe or in Asia. War, famine, drought, and poverty made life difficult for millions of people. Many were hungry and homeless.

The governments of many countries were cruel and harsh. For example, some European governments passed laws to *segregate* Jews. Those laws forced them to live in certain neighborhoods only, apart from others. They were denied the rights that others had.

In many countries, people were put in prison, tortured, or murdered because of their political beliefs.

Millions of people left Europe and Asia to seek a better life in the United States. Some came looking for land or jobs. Many came to find political or religious freedom.

During the 1840s, a large wave of immigrants arrived on America's east coast. They came mostly from northern and western Europe, from countries such as Ireland, England, France, Germany, and Sweden. They settled on farms in the Mississippi Valley. They also settled in the cities of the North.

On the west coast, thousands of immigrants arrived from China. The Chinese worked in the mining camps of California and laid down tracks for western railroads.

Emma Lazarus was the daughter of a Jewish immigrant. She worked to improve the lives of immigrants. In 1883, she wrote a poem about the Statue of Liberty. The words below are from that poem. They are engraved on a plaque at the base of the statue.

"Give me your tired, your poor,
Your huddled masses yearning to breathe free,
The wretched refuse from your teeming shore.
Send these, the homeless, tempest-tost to me,
I lift my lamp beside the golden door!"

AP/Wide World Photos

A New Wave of Immigrants

Beginning in the 1870s, a second large wave of immigrants arrived in the United States. Many of them came from southern and eastern Europe.

The largest group of new immigrants came from Italy. The next largest group were Jews from eastern Europe, most of whom had fled from Russia to find religious freedom and jobs. The third largest group were Slavs from Russia, the Ukraine, Poland, Croatia, Serbia, Bulgaria, and Bohemia. Other immigrants came from Greece, Portugal, Armenia, Turkey, Mexico, China, and Japan.

Leaving Home for America

To get to America, the immigrants crossed the Atlantic or Pacific Ocean on crowded steamships. Many came the cheapest way possible, as *steerage* passengers. Steerage passengers stayed in areas near the engines and the rudders of the ships.

Most Europeans entered the United States through **Ellis Island**, the port of entry in New York harbor. Asians entered through **Angel Island**, the port of entry in San Francisco Bay.

In 1886, the Statue of Liberty was raised in New York harbor. The statue became a symbol to arriving immigrants. It stood for the promise of a new land and a new beginning.

Starting a New Life as Americans

The new immigrants settled mainly in the cities. Most of them were very poor. They crowded into city *slums* (run-down and overcrowded areas) and took whatever jobs they could get. They worked for long hours and low pay.

The immigrants worked in steel mills, laid railroad track, dug coal in mines, sewed clothes, cleaned streets, and worked in slaughterhouses, stockyards, textile mills, and factories. They helped build up America's industries.

Looking Back

1. Why did millions of people leave Europe and Asia in the 1800s?
2. What were immigrants to the United States looking for?
3. What hardships did immigrants face on the voyage to America?
4. What jobs did new immigrants find in America?

Workers Fight for Better Lives

Before 1800, most Americans worked for themselves. They were farmers, or they ran small businesses such as a store or a carpenter's shop. They might hire a few people who worked for wages.

When industries developed, ways of making a living changed. Most people no longer worked for themselves or for small businesses. Instead, they made their living by working for large corporations. They worked for wages in huge mills, canneries, and factories.

A Hard Way to Make a Living

Most industries paid wages that were very low. So, working for wages was a difficult way for people to make a living. In order to survive, everyone in a family went to work, including very young children. Even when every member of the family worked, many families had barely enough to live on.

During economic depressions, many businesses lost money. The owners of those businesses would then lay off some of their workers. Workers who were not laid off were given less pay than before.

Workers could not be sure of keeping their jobs even when business was good. Manufacturers laid off workers when their companies had made enough of certain products. Sometimes, workers were hired for only short periods of time.

Bad Working Conditions

Many factories and mills were kept running day and night. Hundreds or thousands of people worked each *shift* (set of work hours). Most of the work was done with machines. Workers were expected to work faster and faster. Men, women, and children worked 10 to 13 hours a day, six days a week.

Library of Congress

In the 1800s, children worked alongside adults in factories. This photograph shows a young worker in a textile factory.

Working conditions were unhealthy and unsafe. Factories were cold in the winter and hot in summer. They did not have enough light. Often, the machines used were dangerous. Many workers were injured or killed in accidents.

The Rise of Labor Unions

Workers usually took whatever the owners of a company offered. Workers could not ask for higher pay, shorter working hours, or safer working conditions. If the workers thought they were treated unfairly, they often were afraid to complain. Workers who complained were usually fired.

Workers began to realize that they needed to join together. Alone, they had no power against company owners. But together they could refuse to work—go on *strike*—until the owners gave them what they asked for. They began to form workers' organizations. Those organizations were the first American *labor unions*.

In 1886, the **American Federation of Labor (AFL)** was formed. A federation is an organization of groups that join together to support each other. The AFL was an organization of unions. The workers in each union did the same kind of work. For example, plumbers were in one union. Printers were in another. And iron and steel workers were in another.

Organized Labor
Proud and Free

USA 15¢

This U.S. postage stamp honors labor unions.

Collective Bargaining

The AFL tried to get what workers wanted through **collective bargaining**.

Here is an example of collective bargaining: Suppose that workers at a company want higher pay. They all belong to a union. People who represent that union and people who represent the company meet together. The union representatives tell the company how much pay the workers want. The company representatives say how much the company is willing to pay.

If the two sides do not agree, they *bargain*. Each side tries to get the best deal it can. But the two sides also try to reach a compromise. To do that, the union might agree to accept less than it asked for. And the company might agree to pay more than it first said it would.

If the two sides cannot reach an agreement, the workers may decide to strike. In that case, they will not work until the company reaches an agreement with them.

Companies Fight the Unions

In the 1880s and 1890s, unions went on hundreds of strikes. The companies fought to *break* (defeat) the unions. In most cases, the companies won over the strikers by hiring *strikebreakers* (non-union workers) to do the jobs of the striking workers. Or companies waited out strikes. When strikers ran out of money, they had to go back to work.

Some strikes were violent. Battles broke out between strikebreakers and striking workers. Companies hired guards or called in state or federal troops who fought the strikers. Many people were injured or killed in the fighting.

The Homestead Strike

One of the most violent strikes was at the Carnegie steel *plant* (factory) in Homestead, Pennsylvania. In 1892, the company cut the wages of the workers at the plant. The iron and steel workers' union planned a strike against the company.

The company hired strikebreakers. A wire fence was put up around the plant to keep out the strikers. Then 300 guards were hired to protect the strikebreakers and the plant.

The guards were brought to the plant in the middle of the night. But the workers found out they were coming. The furious workers met the guards and a violent battle broke out. Sixteen people were killed.

The Pennsylvania National Guard then surrounded the plant and arrested strikers. The strike continued for over four months. It ended when the strikers ran out of money. The company took back some of the workers. But it refused to hire back strikers who belonged to the iron and steel union. The union was broken.

The defeat of the union at Homestead made it difficult for unions in the years ahead. It took more than 20 years for unions to become strong.

Looking Back

1. How did the growth of industries change the way people made a living?
2. What was factory work like in the 1800s?
3. How did workers try to improve their wages and working conditions?
4. How did companies fight the unions?

Problems in American Government and Life

As industry grew in America, serious problems also grew. The owners of industry became rich and powerful. They used their wealth to bribe corrupt government leaders. At the same time, many Americans, especially workers in the cities, were living in poverty.

Corruption in Government

Corruption was a problem in state and federal government after the Civil War. It continued after reconstruction was over.

Most city and state governments of the mid-1800s were controlled by a few powerful politicians. They used illegal business deals to make money. For example, New York City was controlled by **William** (*Boss*) **Tweed**. Through bribery and threats, Tweed and his supporters (the *Tweed Ring*) gained control of the city government. Money that was voted to build hospitals and to help the poor went instead to make the Tweed Ring rich.

In the federal government, the *spoils system* led to more corruption. That was the system of giving public jobs as political rewards. After a presidential election, most workers in federal jobs were fired. The new President then appointed friends, relatives, and party supporters to those jobs.

Most people appointed through the spoils system did not have the training to do their jobs. And some were dishonest. They used their jobs to become rich.

Business Leaders Control American Life

Corruption in business was also a problem. Big businesses owned most of the country's wealth. Their leaders used money to bribe or pressure government officials. In that way, big business could control what laws were passed.

Businesses were beginning to control American life. They gained monopolies on products that were necessary for living and then set high prices for those products. The cost of living rose. Some Americans could no longer buy the things they needed.

Businesses were polluting air and rivers with wastes from factories and mills. They also continued to pay low wages to the workers whose long hours of hard work made the business leaders rich.

Cities' Problems Grow

Problems in cities became worse. Roads, sewers, and buildings needed improvement. Drinking water was not safe. Crime increased—especially in the poor areas.

Poor areas of the cities had the most problems. Tenements there were fire hazards. They had no heat or running water, they were overcrowded, and they were infested by rats.

There was no public health care system, so many children in poor areas of the cities were sickly. A study done in Chicago found that more than half the babies in one area died before they were a year old.

Many of the children who did survive left school as soon as they were old enough to work. Sometimes, children as young as five years of age were put to work to help support their family. They had no chance to receive an education, so they had no hope of ever getting a job that paid well. They faced a lifetime of hard work and poverty.

Looking Back

1. How were government and business corrupt?
2. What was the spoils system?
3. What problems did cities face in industrial America?

In the 1800s, many poor families lived in city slums. The family here lived in this one room.

Reformers Work to Solve Problems

Reformers had seen problems in America and had been working to solve them since the early 1800s. Near the end of the 1800s, groups of government and social reformers began to work together. Those reformers believed that *progress* (changes to improve life) could be made. They were called **progressives** for that reason.

Social Reforms Improve People's Lives

Some reformers worked for **social reform**. They helped the poor by working on such social problems as poverty and lack of health care. Social reformers worked to get city governments to clean up slums and improve housing. They also worked to improve life for city children.

Jane Addams was a leader of social reform. She moved into a Chicago slum. There, she opened a *settlement house* in 1889 called **Hull House**. A settlement house is a community center. It offers many kinds of free services. Hull House workers took care of children so that mothers could work. Hull House teachers gave classes in English and health. And there was free medical care.

By 1900, there were over 100 settlement houses like Hull House in poor city neighborhoods.

Political Reforms Control Corruption

Progressives believed that one way to improve government was to give the people more of a voice in running it. The people could then get rid of corrupt officials and keep them out of office.

Progressives worked for political reforms such as the **recall**, **primary election**, and **initiative**.

The *recall* is a special election in which people can vote to remove an official from office. For example, if people decide their mayor is harming the city, they can vote to remove him or her.

In a *primary election*, people in each political party vote for the candidates who will run for government offices. Party leaders used to make those choices.

An *initiative* is a suggestion for a state law that comes from the people, instead of the state legislature. People vote on the initiative in an election. If the majority vote for it, the initiative becomes law.

Reforms in the Federal Government

In 1881, the new President, **James Garfield**, was assassinated. He was killed by a man who had not been given a job through the spoils system. **Chester Arthur**, who then became President, and Congress worked to bring about reforms.

They passed the **Civil Service Act of 1883**. That Act created the *civil service system*. Under that system, people who want government jobs must pass tests to prove they can do the jobs. Once hired, they are not let go after elections.

Looking Back
1. What did social reformers do to improve people's lives?
2. How did progressives reform government?
3. How did the civil service system help control the spoils system?

The Right to Vote–
Progress and Problems

Some reformers saw problems in America involving the right to vote. The reformers tried to solve those problems. Reformers worked to make sure there were voting rights for two groups of Americans: women and Blacks.

Women Fight for the Right to Vote

Women had first demanded the right to vote in the 1840s. But those women had little support. At that time, most people believed that a woman's place was at home. They believed that women understood little about life outside the home—in the "man's world" of politics, government, and business.

Some women did not accept that view, and they continued to fight for the right to vote. After the Civil War, some women began to organize a women's *suffrage* movement. (Suffrage means *vote.*) Those *suffragettes* organized in every state.

Some States Give Women the Vote

The suffragettes' early victories were in the West. In 1870, Wyoming became first to give all women the right to vote. By 1900, women were voting in Idaho, Utah, and Colorado as well.

Suffragettes Fight for
a Voting Amendment

By 1910, suffragettes such as **Carrie Chapman Catt** and **Alice Paul** were pressuring Congress. They wanted an amendment added to the Constitution to give women the right to vote throughout the country. Women marched through the streets of Washington, D.C., and spoke again and again with members of Congress. But women would have to wait ten more years before winning their goal.

Some Blacks Lose the Right to Vote

The Fifteenth Amendment gave Blacks the right to vote in 1870. But in the 1890s, southern states found ways to keep Blacks from voting.

Some states began to force Blacks to pass a *literacy test* before voting. A literacy test proves whether or not a person can read. Many Blacks had never learned to read, so they failed the test.

Some states charged a *poll tax*—a fee that a person must pay before voting. Most Blacks in the South were poor. They could not afford to pay the poll tax.

Blacks Are Segregated

Southern states also passed laws to segregate Blacks from Whites. For example, Blacks were not allowed to mix with Whites on railroad cars. Blacks could not go into restaurants or theaters used by Whites. Blacks and Whites had separate schools, parks, prisons, and graveyards.

The NAACP Is Organized

Reformers of both races were outraged by the attempts to control Blacks and take away their voting rights. They began to fight to restore freedom and rights for Blacks.

In 1909, **W.E.B. Du Bois**, a Black historian and educator, helped found the **National Association for the Advancement of Colored People** (NAACP). The group began a fight for civil rights reforms—a fight that has continued into the present.

Looking Back
1. How did suffragettes work for women's right to vote?
2. How did southern states keep Blacks from voting?
3. What is the NAACP?

Chapter 18

Facts First

Complete each sentence, by choosing the correct ending.

1. During the 1800s, the United States
   a. did not allow immigrants into the nation.
   b. received millions of immigrants.
   c. allowed only immigrants from Europe.
2. To reach America, immigrants often
   a. traveled on crowded steamships.
   b. paid a lot to travel in comfort.
   c. flew by airplane.
3. Most immigrants settled
   a. on farms.
   b. in small towns.
   c. in cities.
4. Most immigrants worked
   a. on farms.
   b. in mines, factories, and mills.
   c. at easy jobs that paid a lot of money.
5. To improve their working conditions, workers
   a. went on strikes and joined labor unions.
   b. opened their own businesses.
   c. went to work on farms.
6. Their pay and working conditions made immigrants
   a. rich and comfortable.
   b. poor, sickly, and overworked.
   c. well educated and well paid.
7. Progressives were people who
   a. worked to improve life in America.
   b. fought against social reform.
   c. got rich from corruption in government.
8. Suffragettes were women
   a. who suffered from poverty.
   b. who worked for women's voting rights.
   c. who became strikebreakers.

Word Check

Write the meanings of these words. Then use them in sentences.

ethnic	segregate
labor union	strike

Skill Builder

Find out about one of the reformers below. Then report what you learned.

Jane Addams	Robert La Follette, Sr.
Carrie Chapman Catt	Jacob Riis
W.E.B. Du Bois	Upton Sinclair
Samuel Gompers	Lincoln Steffens

Chapter 18 Notes

Read over the chapter. Find answers to these questions:

1. Describe the life of an immigrant in an American city of the late 1800s.
2. How did collective bargaining sometimes help factory and mill workers?
3. Explain each of these reforms:
   a. recall
   b. primary election
   c. initiative
4. How did some states try to keep Blacks separate from Whites?

Be a Historian

Interview someone who belongs to a union. (Teachers, custodians, cafeteria workers, and factory workers often belong to unions.) Ask that person these questions:

1. What union do you belong to?
2. What kinds of workers belong to your union?
3. What do you like about being a union member?

Unit 6

Review

What Do You Know?

Use words below to complete each sentence.

competition   reformers
Great Plains   reservations
immigrants   towns
labor unions   transportation
railroads   vote

1. Thousands of settlers were carried west by _____ during the late 1800s.
2. Many western _____ grew up along the railroads.
3. Farming on the _____ became possible because of inventions such as the steel plow.
4. Plains Indians were forced to move onto _____.
5. New kinds of _____, such as the automobile, changed the way Americans traveled.
6. Some companies formed trusts to try to end _____.
7. Millions of _____ from Europe and Asia came to America seeking a better life.
8. Workers formed _____ to fight for better pay and working conditions.
9. People who worked to end corruption in government were called _____.
10. Suffragettes helped women win the right to _____.

What Do You Think?

Poverty is still a serious problem in America today. The government spends millions of tax dollars to help the poor lead better lives. Some people argue that the government is doing too much to help the poor. They believe the poor should do more to help themselves. What do you think?

Skill Builder

Between 1867 and 1912, 12 states entered the Union. Those states are listed below. (Abbreviations are shown after their names.)

Make a map of the United States showing those states. Write the name or abbreviation of each state on the map. Also write the year each state entered the Union.

- Nebraska (NE) 1867
- Colorado (CO) 1876
- North Dakota (ND) 1889
- South Dakota (SD) 1889
- Montana (MT) 1889
- Washington (WA) 1889
- Idaho (ID) 1890
- Wyoming (WY) 1890
- Utah (UT) 1896
- Oklahoma (OK) 1907
- New Mexico (NM) 1912
- Arizona (AZ) 1912

Unit 6 Notes

Look over the unit to find answers to these questions:

1. How were railroads important to the settlers and towns of the American West?
2. What made it possible for settlers to farm the Great Plains?
3. How did inventions like the electric light, telephone, and automobile change America?
4. Explain each of these big business terms:
   a. corporation   b. monopoly   c. trust
5. Why did labor unions develop? How did they use collective bargaining?
6. How did reformers improve government and make it more democratic?

Word Builder

Write a story about someone who came to America as an immigrant in the 1800s. Use as many of these key words as you can.

Key Words

ethnic   labor union
homesteader   manufacture
industry   segregate

unit 7 Becoming a World Power

Santiago, Cuba—July 1, 1898

Thousands of American soldiers have come to Cuba to fight in a war against Spain. They are helping the Cuban people win their independence from Spain.

One of the soldiers is Colonel Theodore Roosevelt. Just a few weeks ago, Roosevelt held an important job in the United States government. But when war was declared, Roosevelt quit his job to join the fighting.

Roosevelt put together a regiment to fight in Cuba. He chose the toughest men he knew, including Blacks, Whites, and Indians. Roosevelt's regiment is known as the *Rough Riders*.

Roosevelt and the Rough Riders are fighting the Spanish near the city of Santiago. The Spanish hold the hills surrounding the city. Roosevelt receives his orders: Drive the Spanish from San Juan Hill.

Roosevelt leads the Rough Riders in a charge up the hill. By late afternoon, the Americans have taken San Juan Hill. They give a tired cheer as the American flag is raised.

The story of Theodore Roosevelt and the Rough Riders is soon in all the newspapers in the United States. Theodore Roosevelt becomes an American hero.

In Our Time

By the late 1800s, the United States had grown to be a powerful nation. It began to use its power to help other nations fight for freedom and independence.

Today, the United States is even more powerful than it was in the 1800s. And it is still using its power in other lands. How does the United States use its power in other lands today?

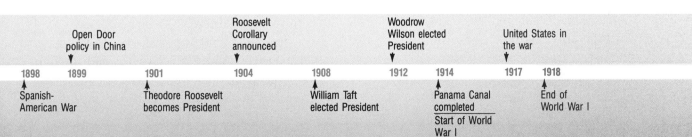

Open Door policy in China		Roosevelt Corollary announced		Woodrow Wilson elected President		United States in the war	
1898	1899	1901	1904	1908	1912	1914	1917	1918
Spanish-American War		Theodore Roosevelt becomes President		William Taft elected President		Panama Canal completed / Start of World War I		End of World War I

Chapter 19 **Becoming an Imperialist Nation**

Manning's Books and Prints, San Francisco

Gold was discovered in Alaska in 1896—and a gold rush began. This photograph from *Harper's Weekly* shows gold prospectors in 1897 Alaska.

During the mid-1800s, many European nations were gaining territories in all parts of the world. But Americans were not interested in expanding into other parts of the world. Instead, they expanded across the American continent. They built railroads and settled the West. They started new businesses and industries.

After the Civil War, the United States began to expand overseas. It increased trade with other nations. And it began to have problems with some nations. By 1898, the United States was at war with Spain.

- How did Alaska become part of the United States?
- How did the United States gain control of Hawaii and other Pacific islands?
- Why did the United States go to war with Spain?

Key Words   You will be using these words in this chapter. Look them up in the glossary at the back of Part 2.

colonialism	**neutral**
isolate	**policy**

America Begins to Look Outward

While America expanded on its own continent, *imperialist* nations of Europe were taking over many parts of Africa and Asia. Those areas became their colonies. (An imperialist nation is one that controls other countries.) The Europeans set up colonial governments to rule their colonies. That system of ruling other lands and peoples is called *colonialism*.

Colonialism gave European nations a steady source of wealth. The overseas colonies provided gold, silver, iron, copper, and other minerals. They also provided *raw materials*, such as wool, lumber, and oil, that European industries use to produce goods.

America Expands into the Pacific

Until the end of the Civil War, the United States government followed a *policy* of isolationism. The government wanted to *isolate* the United States from the rest of the world—keep it out of the affairs and problems of other nations.

Some Americans, however, wanted the United States to expand and become a *world power*—a nation strong enough to deal with the powerful nations of the world.

In 1867, Russia offered to sell Alaska to the United States for $7,200,000. It was a huge area that Russia had claimed in 1741. The area included the Aleutian Islands, a chain of islands that stretched from the coast of Alaska halfway across the Pacific Ocean. Secretary of State **William Seward** convinced Congress to buy Alaska.

In 1896, gold was discovered there. Americans also found Alaska rich in fish, timber, coal, and oil. (Alaska became the nation's 49th state in 1959.)

Manning's Books and Prints, San Francisco

Left: Queen Liliuokalani was the last Hawaiian ruler of the kingdom of Hawaii. *Right*: This engraving from *Harper's Weekly* shows a Hawaiian plantation scene in 1888.

Americans Want Pacific Islands

Since 1784, Americans had traded with the countries of Asia, especially China. They crossed the Pacific on sailing ships. But after the Civil War, they began to use steamships that were powered by engines that burned coal.

The steamships could not carry enough coal to last the journey across the Pacific. Americans wanted islands where ships could stop to refuel.

The United States Annexes Midway and Gains Control of Hawaii

In 1859, American sailors discovered two Pacific islands about halfway between America and Japan. Those islands came to be called *Midway Islands*. In 1867, Secretary of State Seward convinced Congress to annex the islands. Midway became America's first islands in the Pacific.

About a thousand miles from Midway was the island kingdom of Hawaii. It was ruled over by a Hawaiian king or queen.

The location of Hawaii, near the middle of the Pacific, made it a good stopping place for ships traveling to and from Asia. Since the 1780s, ships from many nations, including the United States, had been stopping regularly at Hawaii.

Many Americans had settled on the Hawaiian Islands. Some Americans were *missionaries*—Christians who had come to teach their religion to the Hawaiians. Others were businessmen who started sugar cane plantations or other businesses.

By the late 1800s, sugar cane had become Hawaii's most important crop. Americans controlled most of the land and businesses. In 1887, the Hawaiians allowed the United States to set up a naval base at Pearl Harbor, on the main Hawaiian island of Oahu.

The United States Annexes Hawaii

Americans and other foreigners became powerful in the Hawaiian government. In 1893, they led a rebellion against the Hawaiian ruler, Queen Liliuokalani. In 1894, they declared Hawaii a republic. American sugar cane planters wanted Hawaii to become a territory of the United States. In 1898, they convinced Congress to annex Hawaii. (Hawaii became the 50th state in 1959.)

Hawaii and Midway were not the only Pacific islands that Americans wanted. By 1900, the United States had gained several island *possessions* (territories) in the Pacific.

Looking Back

1. How did colonialism add to the wealth of European nations?
2. Explain the policy of isolationism.
3. How did the purchase of Alaska add to the wealth of the United States?
4. How did the United States gain control of Hawaii?

Trouble in Cuba

In 1892, **Grover Cleveland**, a Democrat, was elected President for the second time. During his presidency, America's overseas trade increased. Americans began to take a greater interest in happenings in other parts of the world.

Americans became interested in what was happening on the island of Cuba, a Spanish colony in the Caribbean Sea. Cubans were unhappy under Spanish rule. In 1895, the Cubans revolted.

Americans Support the Cuban Revolution

The Spanish governor in Cuba called out the Spanish army to crush the revolution. The army killed and captured thousands of Cuban revolutionaries. The army also put Cuban men, women, and children into *detention camps*, where they were kept prisoner by Spanish troops. Many Cubans died of starvation or disease in those camps.

Many Americans supported the Cuban revolution. They compared Cuba's struggle for independence with America's revolution against Britain in 1776.

Americans were also outraged by stories they read that told how cruel the Spanish were.

Some Americans called for a war against Spain to help free Cuba. But President Cleveland was against war. He believed that the United States should remain *neutral*. He said the United States would stay out of the problems between Cuba and Spain.

Yellow Journalism in News Reporting

1896 was a presidential election year, and Republican **William McKinley** was elected President. Like Cleveland, President McKinley hoped to follow a neutral policy toward the Cuban revolution. But American newspapers were stirring up Americans.

In the 1890s, Americans got most of their news from newspapers. There were many newspapers to choose from, and competition among the different newspapers was heavy. To attract more readers, newspapers often printed *sensational* stories—stories that made news events seem more exciting than they really were. Newspapers also printed stories that were untrue. Printing stories that are sensational and untrue is called **yellow journalism**.

Newspapers Stir Up Talk of War

Throughout 1897 and 1898, two of the nation's largest newspapers, the *New York World* and the *New York Journal*, were competing for readers. Both papers were filled with sensational stories of the ways the Spanish mistreated Cubans. One story reported that women and children who died in detention camps were "hauled away by garbage collectors in large ox carts." Another story appeared under this headline: "FEEDING PRISONERS TO SHARKS."

Day after day, Americans read about freedom-loving Cubans who were killed or mistreated by Spanish troops. Some of the stories were made up. But many people believed they were true. By 1898, many Americans were calling for war.

Looking Back
1. Why did Americans support Cuba in its fight for independence?
2. What is yellow journalism? How did it cause people to want to go to war against Spain?
3. Do you think magazines or newspapers today practice yellow journalism? Why do you think that?

Library of Congress
The front page of The New York World

The Spanish-American War (1898)

At the time of the Cuban revolution, many Americans lived in Havana, the capital city of Cuba. In 1898, fighting broke out there. President McKinley sent the battleship *Maine* to Havana to protect American citizens. On February 15, a huge explosion destroyed the *Maine*.

The cause of the explosion was never known, but American newspapers blamed Spain for it. Furious Americans insisted that Congress declare war against Spain. They used the slogan ''Remember the *Maine*!'' to win supporters. In April 1898, Congress declared war against Spain.

Victory in the Philippines

America did not fight the first battle of the war in Cuba. Instead, the first battle was fought in the Philippines, a group of 7000 islands in Southeast Asia. The Philippines had been colonized by Spain. As in Cuba, rebels in the Philippines were fighting to be free from Spain.

On May 1, an American fleet attacked a Spanish fleet in Manila harbor in the Philippines. The entire Spanish fleet was sunk.

Another American fleet took control of Wake Island and the Spanish island of Guam in the Pacific. That fleet then arrived in Manila harbor to join the Americans there. On August 13, 1898, they captured Manila, the capital, and took the Philippines.

Victory in Cuba

In June 1898, an American army invaded Cuba. Nearly 20,000 American troops landed near Santiago, in southeastern Cuba. On July 1, the Americans drove the Spanish from the hills near the city. (The story you read at the beginning of this chapter is about the fighting around Santiago. It was during those battles that **Theodore Roosevelt** and the Rough Riders captured San Juan Hill.)

Two days later, American ships destroyed a Spanish fleet leaving Santiago harbor. That victory brought an end to the fighting in Cuba.

In late July, American forces took control of Puerto Rico, another Spanish island in the Caribbean Sea. In August, the defeated Spanish asked for peace. The war had lasted just four months.

The Peace Treaty Gives America an Empire

In December 1898, the United States and Spain signed a peace treaty. The treaty made Cuba an independent nation. It gave the United States control of the Philippines, Guam, and Puerto Rico.

Many Americans—including Andrew Carnegie, Jane Addams, and **Mark Twain**—spoke out against the treaty. They said that the United States should not own colonies because it went against American belief in self-government.

Looking Back

1. How did the explosion of the battleship *Maine* lead to war against Spain in 1898?
2. Why were the people of the Philippines fighting against Spain in 1898?
3. What did the United States gain from the Spanish-American War?

156 / *The UNITED STATES*

Governing America's New Empire

As you read, the United States won control of Guam, Puerto Rico, and the Philippines at the end of the Spanish-American War. Guam was a small island, with few people living on it. The United States planned to use it as a naval base, so Guam was placed under navy control.

Puerto Rico was a large island that had first been settled by the Spanish in 1508. Around one million people were living there at the time the United States took control. And the Philippines was a country of many islands and many people. Like Puerto Rico, it had been ruled by Spain since the 1500s. How would the United States govern those islands?

Americans Disagree about the Islands

Americans disagreed about who should govern Puerto Rico and the Philippines. Some Americans said that the United States stood for independence and self-government; therefore, Congress should declare Puerto Rico and the Philippines independent nations. Then the Puerto Ricans and the people of the Philippines, the *Filipinos*, could govern themselves.

But President McKinley disagreed. He said that Puerto Ricans and Filipinos were not experienced in government because Spain had governed them for so long. Therefore, they were not ready to govern themselves, and the United States should rule them until they learned to rule themselves. The Senate made Puerto Rico and the Philippines United States possessions.

Filipinos Resist United States Control

When the United States defeated Spain, Filipinos had expected to gain independence. When that did not happen, they rebelled.

America's fight against the Filipinos was much longer than its war against Spain. Finally, in 1901, American troops defeated the Filipinos. America had won control of the Philippines, but the cost was high: at least 4000 Americans and 200,000 Filipinos had lost their lives.

Governing the Philippines

An American governor was put in charge of the Philippines. Millions of dollars were used to build roads, schools, and hospitals.

Slowly, Filipinos were given the power to govern themselves. A legislature was set up. By 1916, Filipinos were electing all its members. But it was not until 1946—after over 40 years of American rule—that the United States granted independence to the Philippines.

Governing Puerto Rico

The people of Puerto Rico did not resist American rule. The first American governor was sent to the island in 1900. In 1917, the people of Puerto Rico were made United States citizens. They were allowed to elect a legislature that ruled with the governor.

In 1952, Puerto Rico became a *commonwealth* of the United States. As a commonwealth, Puerto Rico governs itself. But it is not an independent nation: Its people are American citizens, and Puerto Rico is protected by the United States.

Looking Back

1. How did Americans disagree about governing Puerto Rico and the Philippines?
2. Why did Filipinos fight against the United States in 1899?
3. How did the Philippines become an independent nation?
4. What is Puerto Rico's relationship with the United States today?

Chapter 19

Facts First

Complete each sentence by choosing the correct ending.

empires   Spain
fought   steamships
Hawaii   William Seward
Puerto Rico   yellow journalism

1. In the mid-1800s, many European nations were building _____.
2. _____ convinced Congress to buy Alaska.
3. America wanted islands in the Pacific where _____ could refuel.
4. America annexed _____ after American settlers rebelled against its ruler.
5. Sensational news stories about the Cuban rebellion were called _____.
6. Americans went to war to help free Cuba from _____.
7. The United States won Guam, the Philippines, and _____ in the Spanish-American War.
8. Filipinos _____ against American rule because they wanted independence.

Word Check

Write the meaning of each of these words. Then use each word in a sentence.

colonialism   neutral
isolate   policy

Skill Builder

Show where each of these places is on a map of the world or on a globe. Then choose one of the places. Give a report about what it is like today.

Alaska   Midway Islands
Cuba   Philippine Islands
Guam   Puerto Rico
Hawaii   Wake Island

Chapter 19 Notes

Read over the chapter. Find answers to these questions:

1. How did imperialist nations become richer by controlling colonies?
2. How did the United States gain control of Alaska? of Hawaii?
3. What made Americans call for war against Spain in 1898?
4. How did the United States gain control of the Philippine Islands?
5. Why did Filipinos fight against the United States? Were the Filipinos successful?
6. How did the United States gain control of Puerto Rico? What does it mean when we say that Puerto Rico is a *commonwealth*?

Be a Historian

Americans have been buying foreign-made goods since colonial times. What items in your home were made in other countries? Check the label, sticker, or stamp on some items (like clothes and furniture) to find out.

Make a list of imported items that you find. Next to each item, write the name of the country in which it was made.

Bonus

Call a travel agency for information about Alaska, Hawaii, or Puerto Rico. Ask them to send you information (brochures, posters) about that place. Make a class display with the materials you receive.

Chapter 20 The United States Looks Outward

Historical Pictures Service, Chicago

This political cartoon shows Theodore Roosevelt using his "big stick" policy in the Caribbean.

In 1900, William McKinley was elected to a second term as President. Theodore Roosevelt was elected Vice-President.

In September 1901, President McKinley went to Buffalo, New York, to give an important speech. There, on September 6, the President was shot by an assassin who hid in a line of people waiting to shake his hand. McKinley died eight days later, and Theodore Roosevelt became President.

Under President Roosevelt, the nation became more active in world affairs. Roosevelt believed the United States should "speak softly and carry a big stick" in dealing with other nations. Roosevelt meant that the nation should be ready to use military force ("a big stick") to protect its trade and overseas territories.

- What was the Monroe Doctrine?
- How did relations with Central and South America change under Roosevelt?
- Why did the United States build the Panama Canal?
- How did the United States become involved in the affairs of China and Japan?

Key Words   You will be using these words in this chapter. Look them up in the glossary at the back of Part 2.

    finances   **world affairs**
    isthmus   **zone**

The United States and Latin America

When Theodore Roosevelt became President in 1901, the United States had already shown other nations that it was strong. It had become a world power, involved in **world affairs**.

In 1902, Americans became concerned about what was happening in *Latin America*. (Latin America is made up of all the countries of North and South America that are south of the United States.) Three European nations had sent warships to the Caribbean Sea. Americans thought that those European countries were violating the **Monroe Doctrine**. That was a policy that had been started in 1823 under President James Monroe.

Background of the Monroe Doctrine

You remember that Spain had founded colonies in Central and South America after the discovery of America in 1492. By the early 1800s, most of the colonies had revolted against Spain and had become independent nations.

But in 1823, stories reached America that Spain was planning to take back those colonies with the help of other European nations. At the same time, Russia was building forts along the west coast of North America. President Monroe saw both actions as threats to the United States. He warned the nations of Europe to stay out of American affairs.

The idea that European nations should stay out of the Americas became known as the Monroe Doctrine. The Monroe Doctrine became part of American *foreign policy*. A country's foreign policy is the way its government deals with the governments of other nations.

Roosevelt Takes a Stronger Stand

In 1902, the South American nation of Venezuela owed large sums of money to several European nations. Venezuela was ruled by a dictator who refused to repay those debts. So, Britain, Germany, and Italy sent warships to blockade Venezuela until the debts were paid.

President Roosevelt believed that those European countries had the right to try to get Venezuela to pay its debts. But he and other Americans thought that the blockade violated the Monroe Doctrine.

In 1903, Roosevelt asked the Europeans to end their blockade, and they agreed to do so. Roosevelt then helped Venezuela work out a way to pay its debts.

The problem in Venezuela convinced President Roosevelt that the United States needed a stronger foreign policy in Latin America. Other Latin American countries owed money to European nations. Those nations might use force to collect the debts. Roosevelt did not want European troops and ships in the Americas.

President Roosevelt was also concerned about the weak governments in many Latin American countries. Rebellions took place often in those countries. Roosevelt thought European nations might decide to take over those weak Latin American countries.

The Roosevelt Corollary

In 1904, Roosevelt announced a new foreign policy in Latin America. He said that if a Latin American nation could not keep order within its borders, the United States might have to take action. To Roosevelt, that meant acting like a policeman in the Caribbean and throughout Latin America.

If a nation did not keep peace or pay its debts, the United States could step in. Such action would keep European nations out.

Roosevelt's announcement added a new idea to the Monroe Doctrine. The announcement became known as the **Roosevelt Corollary**. (A corollary is an addition to a statement or document.)

The United States Steps In

Between 1905 and 1935, the United States often made use of the Roosevelt Corollary. For example, in 1905, the United States took control of the *finances* of the Dominican Republic, a small country in the Caribbean. The Dominican Republic owed over $30 million to European nations. American officials took over the job of collecting its import taxes. After several years, the country's debts were paid.

In 1912, United States Marines were sent to Nicaragua, in Central America. The marines put down a rebellion there. Later, American troops were also sent to Haiti and the Dominican Republic to keep order.

Latin Americans Resent U.S. Policy

President Roosevelt believed that the United States was protecting Latin America and bringing peace to the countries there. But Latin Americans had a different view. They resented United States troops in their countries. And they claimed that the United States had no right to interfere in the affairs of independent nations.

Looking Back

1. What did the Monroe Doctrine do?
2. According to the Roosevelt Corollary, what might the United States do if a Latin American country could not keep order within its borders?
3. Why did Latin Americans resent United States foreign policy after 1905?

The Panama Canal

You read about the Spanish-American War in Chapter 19. During that war, the American fleet in the Caribbean sent for help. An American warship named the *Oregon* left San Francisco for the Caribbean Sea. To reach the Caribbean, the *Oregon* had to sail all the way around the tip of South America, a journey of 11,000 miles. When the ship arrived 68 days later, the fighting in the Caribbean was nearly over.

The Need for a Short Route

The journey of the *Oregon* convinced American leaders that they had to find a way to get ships quickly from the Pacific to the Atlantic. In 1902, President Roosevelt and Congress agreed to build a canal connecting the two oceans.

America Makes an Offer

Congress decided that the best place to dig a canal was in Central America, across the *Isthmus of Panama*. That **isthmus** is the narrow strip of land that connects North and South America.

At that time, the South American nation of Colombia controlled Panama. President Roosevelt offered Colombia ten million dollars to buy land across Panama for the canal. But Colombia wanted more money and refused the President's offer.

Panama Revolts Against Colombia

For years, the people of Panama had fought for independence from Colombia. When Colombia refused Roosevelt's offer, he let it be known that the United States would help Panama if it decided to revolt. On November 3, 1903, the people of Panama revolted. American warships kept Colombia's troops from landing in Panama to end the revolt. Panama declared itself an independent nation.

Library of Congress

The Panama Canal was opened in 1914. This ship was one of the first to go through the canal.

America Buys a Canal Zone

Two weeks later, President Roosevelt signed a treaty with the new Republic of Panama. The treaty gave the United States control of a ten-mile-wide strip of land across Panama. That land was called the **Panama Canal Zone**. The United States was given the right to govern that **zone**. In return, the United States agreed to pay Panama ten million dollars, as well as rent of $250,000 per year beginning in 1913.

Controlling Disease in the Canal Zone

The Isthmus of Panama was a dangerous place to live and work: Diseases such as yellow fever and malaria killed thousands of people there every year. Before work on the American canal could begin, those diseases had to be controlled. **William Gorgas** was given the job of controlling diseases in the Canal Zone. He was a doctor in the United States Army.

Gorgas knew that mosquitos spread yellow fever and malaria. So, he and his workers attacked the mosquitos' breeding ground. The workers drained swamps, cut tall grass, and sprayed pools of water with oil. Water barrels were kept covered, and even holy water in churches was changed daily. By 1914, yellow fever and malaria had largely disappeared from Panama.

This U.S. postage stamp was issued on the 25th anniversary of the Panama Canal.

Digging the Canal

In 1907, President Roosevelt put Colonel **George Goethals** in charge of building the canal. Goethals was an engineer in the United States Army.

Building the canal was long, hard, and dangerous work. Workers had to make a massive cut in the earth across nearly 50 miles of jungle, hills, mountains, and swamps. Workers had to blast through rocks and move millions of tons of dirt. Hundreds of workers were killed or injured by accidents.

By 1914, over 43,000 workers from 97 countries had worked on the canal. Most of them were Blacks from the British West Indies. Finally, in the summer of 1914, their job was finished, and the canal was opened. It had taken almost ten years altogether to complete. Newspapers around the world called the Panama Canal "the greatest engineering feat of the ages."

With the Panama Canal completed, the United States could move ships quickly to protect the nation's territories in the Caribbean and the Pacific. *Cargo ships* could also move easily from the east coast of the United States to Asia. (Cargo ships carry goods from one country to another.) The United States allowed ships from all nations to use the canal if they paid a toll.

Panama Promised Control of the Canal Zone

You remember that Panama gave the United States control of the Canal Zone in the treaty of 1903. That meant that the Canal Zone became American territory inside Panama.

Many people in Panama were unhappy with American control of the Canal Zone. They believed the Canal Zone was part of their country.

For many years, Panama worked to regain control of the Canal Zone. In 1977, the United States and Panama signed a new treaty. In that treaty, the United States promised to turn over complete control of the Canal Zone to Panama by the year 2000.

Looking Back

1. Why did the United States want to build a canal across Panama?
2. How did the United States gain control of the Panama Canal Zone?
3. How did the people of Panama feel about United States' control of the Canal Zone? Why?
4. What agreement did the United States make with Panama in 1977?
5. *Map work*: What are the countries of Central America?

American Foreign Policy in Asia

During the early 1900s, the United States wanted to build up trade with the countries in the *Far East*, especially China and Japan. (The Far East is made up of countries in eastern Asia.)

The United States Opens China to Trade

China was the largest nation in the Far East; 400 million people lived there. But it was also a troubled nation. During the 1800s, there were many rebellions among the Chinese people. Millions died, and China's government and military were weakened.

During the 1890s, Britain, Germany, Russia, and Japan took over parts of China. Those nations controlled the trade there. They closed Chinese ports to all ships but their own. The United States feared that it would be cut off from trade with China.

In 1899, United States Secretary of State **John Hay** said that all nations should follow an **Open Door policy** in China. He meant that all parts of China should be open to trade with all nations. Hay sent letters to all nations that controlled ports in China, asking that they agree to the Open Door policy. Because the United States was powerful, the other nations agreed.

United States Convinces Japan to Trade

The United States also wanted to trade with Japan, an island nation located close to China. For hundreds of years, the Japanese refused to allow foreigners into their country. Then, in 1853, Commodore **Matthew Perry** arrived in Japan with a strong American fleet. He convinced Japanese leaders to trade with the other nations of the world.

The other nations were more powerful than Japan. They made trade treaties that were better for them than for Japan.

During the 1800s, Japan became stronger. It improved its economy and systems of government and education. It also built a strong army and navy.

By 1900, Japan was a powerful country, interested in expansion. Japan wanted to gain control of Manchuria, a territory that belonged to China. But Russia was also trying to take control of that area.

Roosevelt Helps End Russian-Japanese War

In 1904, Japan and Russia went to war. The Japanese won several victories at the beginning of the war. But by 1905, both sides were tired of the fighting and were eager for peace. President Roosevelt offered to hold peace talks with both countries.

Leaders from the two countries came to the United States for peace talks. Roosevelt helped Japan and Russia reach a peace agreement. Never before had a President played such an important role in ending an *international dispute*—an argument between countries.

Every year, the *Nobel Peace Prize* is presented in Norway. It is an international award that is given to someone who has done outstanding work for world peace. In 1906, President Roosevelt was given the Nobel Prize for his work as a peacemaker between Russia and Japan.

Looking Back

1. Who controlled trade with China in the 1890s? How?
2. What was the Open Door policy?
3. How did President Roosevelt help end the war between Japan and Russia?
4. Do you think the United States should become involved in the affairs of other nations? Why or why not?

Chapter 20

Review

Facts First

Complete each sentence by choosing the correct ending.

1. The Monroe Doctrine was a warning to
   a. keep out of the Americas.
   b. stop trading with Japan.
   c. keep out of China.
2. President Roosevelt said that if a Latin American country could not pay its debts,
   a. a European nation could take control.
   b. the United States might step in.
   c. the debts would never be repaid.
3. Many Latin American countries
   a. never won their independence.
   b. resented American interference in their affairs.
   c. wanted American soldiers on their soil.
4. The Panama Canal linked
   a. the Gulf of Mexico to the Caribbean Sea.
   b. Colombia to Panama.
   c. the Atlantic Ocean to the Pacific Ocean.
5. The purpose of the Open Door policy was to
   a. divide China into colonies.
   b. open China to American traders.
   c. keep China out of Latin America.
6. President Roosevelt helped Japan to
   a. take over Manchuria.
   b. win a war with China.
   c. end its war with Russia.

Word Check

Write the meanings of these words. Then use them in sentences.

finances	**world affairs**
isthmus	**zone**

Skill Builder

Each of the people below served as President during the years shown. Find out more about one of the Presidents. Then report what you learned.

Rutherford Hayes (1877–1881)
James Garfield (1881)
Chester Arthur (1881–1885)
Grover Cleveland (1885–1889; 1893–1897)
Benjamin Harrison (1889–1893)
William McKinley (1897–1901)
Theodore Roosevelt (1901–1909)
William Taft (1909–1913)

Chapter 20 Notes

Read over the chapter. Find answers to these questions:

1. What was the Monroe Doctrine?
2. What was U.S. foreign policy according to the Roosevelt Corollary?
3. Give two examples of the way America used the Roosevelt Corollary between 1905 and 1935.
4. Why did the United States decide to build a canal connecting the Pacific and Atlantic oceans?
5. What was the Open Door policy?
6. Why did Russia and Japan fight a war in the early 1900s? How did the war end?

Be a Historian

A political cartoon is a drawing by an artist about a news event. Through the cartoon, the artist gives his or her opinion about the news.

Look in recent newspapers and magazines for a political cartoon. Cut out the cartoon and tape it to a sheet of notebook paper. Then write what you think the artist is saying in the cartoon.

Chapter 21 The First World War (1914-1918)

Soldiers fought a new kind of warfare during World War I. These soldiers fighting in France are using new kinds of weapons.

President Theodore Roosevelt served two terms. In 1908, another Republican, **William Taft**, was elected President. President Taft served one term. In 1912, **Woodrow Wilson**, a Democrat, was elected the nation's 28th President.

President Wilson believed that nations should *negotiate* when they had problems: Their leaders should meet to talk together and work out agreements. In that way, he hoped that conflicts could be settled peacefully.

In 1914, war broke out in Europe. President Wilson tried to keep the United States out of the war. But by 1917, United States soldiers were fighting in Europe.

- Why did the nations of Europe go to war?
- How did the United States become involved in the war?
- How did the government organize the nation for war?
- What happened at the end of the war?

Key Words   You will be using these words in this chapter. Look them up in the glossary at the back of Part 2.

    draft   relations
    markets   technology

Competition and Tension in Europe

In Chapter 19, you read that many European nations were building empires in the late 1800s. They competed for new colonies and for *markets* in other countries. Competition sometimes resulted in war. So, European nations built up large armies and navies. They also found *allies*—nations that they could count on for help. They formed alliances with those nations: They agreed to help each other fight in case of war.

The two great imperialist nations of Europe were Germany and Britain. Germany formed an alliance with Austria-Hungary. Britain formed an alliance with France and Russia. By 1914, those alliances had split Europe into two opposing sides.

The alliances of 1914 were dangerous for the whole world: If any two nations fought, their allies would have to fight too. Since the nations had empires all over the world, the war could spread all over the world. It could become a *world war*, with many different nations fighting in many parts of the world.

One of President Wilson's advisors was William House. In 1914, House visited Germany and sent a report back to the President. He warned that the situation in Europe was dangerous. He said that unless President Wilson found a way to improve the situation, war was sure to come.

Looking Back

1. What were Britain and Germany competing for in the late 1800s?
2. Why did European nations form alliances with other countries?
3. The United States has alliances with many nations today. Do you think that is a good idea? Why or why not?

The War Begins

The event that started the First World War took place in Sarajevo, a city in Austria-Hungary. Austria-Hungary was a country in central Europe. (It later split into the two countries of Austria and Hungary.) Archduke Francis Ferdinand was visiting Sarajevo. The archduke was the *heir* (next in line) to the throne of Austria-Hungary.

Assassination Brings War

On June 28, 1914, an assassin shot and killed the archduke. The assassin was part of a group of terrorists in Serbia, a country south of Austria-Hungary, so Austria-Hungary declared war on Serbia.

Russia was an ally of Serbia, and it sent troops to help fight Austria-Hungary. Since Austria-Hungary was part of the German alliance, Germany declared war on Russia. Since Russia was part of the British alliance, Britain and France then declared war on Germany and Austria-Hungary.

By September, almost all the nations of Europe had taken sides. Those on the side of Germany and Austria-Hungary were called the **Central Powers**. Those fighting with Russia, France, and Britain were known as the **Allied Powers**, or the **Allies**.

Europeans Fight a New Kind of War

In the first months of the war, German troops marched through Belgium and into France. In France, the Germans were stopped by Allied troops. Both sides dug long lines of deep *trenches*, or ditches, to fight from. Soldiers fired at each other from the trenches and tried to take their enemy's trenches. From overhead, airplanes dropped bombs and poison gas into the trenches.

Air and chemical warfare were new to the world. They came about because of new ***technology*** that made it possible to invent deadlier weapons than those of the past. Hundreds of thousands of soldiers on both sides died in the trenches in France.

The United States Remains Neutral

In 1914, President Wilson declared that the United States would not take sides in the fighting. The President said the war had nothing to do with America. He asked Americans to be neutral "in thought as well as action."

But it was difficult for Americans not to take sides. Many Americans had been born in Europe, or their parents or grandparents were from Europe. Many Americans had friends and relatives living in Europe. Many Americans also disliked the German government because it was not a democracy; it was ruled by a powerful emperor.

Some Americans sided with Germany and the Central Powers. But most Americans sided with Britain, France, and the other Allies—nations that the United States had friendly ***relations*** with.

Americans were also influenced by British *propaganda*—information that is given in such a way that people see things from a certain point of view. British newspapers sent stories to America describing Germany as a power-hungry country. The stories said that Germany was trying to expand its empire by taking over all democratic nations of the world. German soldiers were described as cruel and bloodthirsty.

Looking Back

1. What event started the war in Europe?
2. Why did the war become a world war?
3. What was United States policy toward the war when it broke out?

The *Lusitania*, a passenger ship, was sunk by the Germans in 1915.

America Goes to War

The war in Europe created a business boom in the United States. The Central Powers and the Allies bought steel, oil, food, ammunition, and other war supplies from the United States. In 1914 alone, the Allies and Central Powers spent over one billion dollars for American goods.

But trade with the Allies and Central Powers also caused problems for the United States.

Britain Stops American Ships

By late 1914, Britain's navy had set up a blockade of German ports. The blockade was effective: German merchant ships could not reach the United States to take on supplies. And British warships stopped American ships carrying supplies for Germany. The British forced American ships into British ports, sometimes holding them for weeks. The British seized any war supplies they found on American ships.

Although the British paid for the goods they seized, the United States protested. The United States claimed that, as a neutral nation, it had the right to trade with any country. But Britain ignored the protests and continued to stop American ships heading for Germany.

U-boats Attack Allied Ships

American officials were angry with Britain for interfering with American trade. But they soon had a more serious complaint against Germany.

In 1915, Germany tried to cut off Allied trade with America by using a new kind of warship—the *U-boat*, or submarine. German U-boats moved underwater, where they could not be seen. They attacked any Allied ship they found, including unarmed merchant and passenger ships. Hundreds of Allied ships were sunk and thousands of passengers and crew members died in U-boat attacks.

Americans were outraged by Germany's submarine warfare. Americans protested that U-boat attacks violated *international law*. (International law refers to rules that nations are expected to follow. Several countries had agreed on a set of wartime rules in the *Geneva Convention* of 1864.)

According to international law, a ship was supposed to warn another ship before attacking it. That gave the crew and passengers a chance to escape in lifeboats. Ships were then expected to rescue passengers and crew members from the water. But U-boats attacked without warning and made no effort to rescue anyone.

The Sinking of the Lusitania

On May 7, 1915, a U-boat sank a British passenger ship near Ireland. The ship was the *Lusitania*. When it sank, 1,198 people were killed, including 128 Americans.

President Wilson sent an angry letter to Germany's leaders. He demanded an apology for the attack on the *Lusitania* and an end to submarine warfare against unarmed merchant and passenger ships. Germany apologized, but the attacks continued.

In March 1916, Germany attacked a French passenger ship, the *Sussex*. President Wilson again protested. Germany did not want war with the United States. So, it agreed to stop attacking unarmed ships without warning.

Relations with Germany Grow Worse

In 1916, Woodrow Wilson won a second term as President. His campaign slogan was, "He kept us out of war!" After his election, Wilson tried to end the war. He asked the Allies and Central Powers to accept a "peace without victory." They refused.

At that time, America's trade with the Allies had reached over three billion dollars. American bankers were lending England and France large amounts of money. To Germany, it seemed that the United States was not neutral at all.

In January 1917, Germany announced that it was setting up a submarine blockade: Germany would sink any ship, neutral or enemy, that tried to reach Britain.

President Wilson cut off relations with Germany. But he still hoped to avoid war. Then, in March, President Wilson learned about the **Zimmerman note**. It was a secret message that had been sent to the government of Mexico. The British had gotten a copy of it and had given it to the United States.

The note had been sent by Arthur Zimmerman, a high German official. In the note, Zimmerman proposed that Mexico form an alliance with Germany to fight the United States. After the war, Mexico would receive Texas, New Mexico, and Arizona as a reward for its help.

Americans were shocked and angry about the Zimmerman note. Then came the news: German U-boats had sunk three American ships. War could no longer be avoided.

The United States Declares War

On April 2, President Wilson spoke to Congress. He asked Congress to declare war on Germany and its allies.

President Wilson said that the United States could not allow Germany to sink American ships—America must fight for "freedom of the seas." By that, he meant that the United States must fight for its right to trade with any nation it chose. Wilson also said the "world must be made safe for democracy." He meant that a German victory might mean the end of democratic nations such as Britain and the United States.

On April 6, 1917, Congress voted to declare war on Germany and its allies.

Looking Back

1. How did the war help business in America?
2. Why were Americans outraged by submarine warfare?
3. What events led America to declare war against Germany?
4. What reasons did President Wilson give for declaring war on Germany?
5. *Map work*: On a map, find Germany, France, and Britain.

America Prepares to Fight

The United States was not prepared for war in 1917. The American army had only about 200,000 troops. The nation was also short of military supplies. President Wilson and Congress acted quickly to *mobilize* the nation—prepare it for war.

Building an Army

Congress passed the **Selective Service Act** in May 1917. That law said that all men 21 to 30 years old must register for the *draft*. (A draft is a system for ordering people to serve in the armed forces.)

During the Civil War, many Americans had opposed a draft. They said it was wrong to force people to serve in the armed forces. But in 1917, most Americans supported the draft. Millions of American men quickly registered. In 1917 and 1918, nearly three million Americans were drafted. Another two million volunteered for the armed forces. By the end of the war, the United States had raised an army of nearly five million troops.

The Government Controls Industry

In Chapter 17, you read that the government does not control industry under the free enterprise system. But in 1917, the nation faced a great crisis. The government had to make sure that America's factories produced the weapons and supplies needed to win the war.

In 1917, President Wilson created the **War Industries Board**. The board was a wartime government office. It had the power to control factories that produced important war materials, such as steel, rubber, and oil. The board also controlled factories that produced weapons, ammunition, and uniforms.

The War Industries Board decided what goods were needed and made sure factories produced those goods. It also told factory owners how much they could charge for their goods. Within months, the nation's factories were steadily producing guns, bullets, uniforms, and other needed supplies.

The Government Controls Food Production

The government also took control of America's food production. More food was needed for America's growing army and for Allied soldiers. Food was also needed for starving *civilians* in war areas overseas. (Civilians are people who are not in any military force.)

President Wilson set up another government office, the **Food Administration**, to increase farm production. Wilson put **Herbert Hoover** in charge of the Food Administration. Hoover promised farmers that the government would pay high prices for wheat, sugar cane, and other crops. That promise encouraged farmers to plant more of those crops.

Hoover also encouraged Americans to use less wheat, meat, and other foods that could be sent overseas. Those foods were sent to American soldiers and the Allies. Hoover called for "wheatless Mondays" and "porkless Thursdays." On those days, Americans were asked to eat no wheat or pork products. Americans were also encouraged to grow their own vegetables at home in "victory gardens."

Hoover's efforts were a success. In 1918, the United States nearly tripled the amount of food it sent to the Allies.

The U.S. government issued patriotic posters like this during World War I.

FOOD WILL WIN THE WAR
You came here seeking Freedom
You must now help to preserve it
WHEAT is needed for the allies
Waste nothing

Library of Congress

Paying for the War

The cost of fighting Germany and its allies was huge. The government needed money to pay its soldiers and to pay for war supplies. It also needed to lend money to the Allies. The Allies had been fighting for three years; they had spent nearly all the money they had.

To raise money, the government increased **income taxes**. (Income taxes are taxes people and businesses pay to the government. Those taxes are based on the amount of money earned.)

The government also sold **war bonds** to the American people. When Americans bought a war bond, they were lending the government the amount of money the bond was worth. After the war, people could cash in the bond for its value, plus interest. The government raised over 21 billion dollars by selling war bonds.

Support for the War

The government could not raise taxes, sell war bonds, and carry out other wartime plans without the support of Americans. So, President Wilson set up the **Committee on Public Information (CPI)**. That was an office whose job was to stir up patriotism and loyalty.

The CPI printed pamphlets and posters that supported America's fight against Germany. CPI workers gave patriotic speeches in movie theaters and meeting halls. Actors and other famous people encouraged Americans to buy war bonds. Movie directors made war movies about brave people who fought and died in the war against Germany.

Laws Control People Against the War

Most Americans supported the war, but a small number of Americans did not. Many of those who did not were loyal Americans who believed that wars for any reason are wrong. Because of their beliefs, they refused to fight.

But the government wanted to make sure that no one would damage the war effort. In 1917, Congress passed the **Espionage Act**: Anyone found guilty of aiding the enemy could be sentenced to 20 years in jail. In 1918, Congress passed the **Sedition Act**: Anyone who spoke out against the government, the Constitution, the American flag, or the military could be punished.

During the war, over 1500 people were arrested for violating the Espionage Act or the Sedition Act.

Looking Back

1. How did the United States build up its army?
2. Why did the government take control of many American industries?
3. How did the government pay for the war?
4. What was the Espionage Act? the Sedition Act?
5. Do you think it is right to punish people who speak out against the government in time of war? Why or why not?

The Allied Victory

When the United States entered the war, the American navy moved quickly to end the threat of the German U-boats. American troop ships would soon be carrying thousands of soldiers to fight in Europe. Those ships had to be protected from U-boat attacks.

In 1917, American and British naval commanders set up a *convoy system* to protect supply ships. In the convoy system, supply ships traveled together in a tight group, or *convoy*. Warships traveled with the supply ships, protecting them from submarine attacks.

The convoy system worked well. More and more supply ships reached Britain. The convoy system was so effective that when American troop ships began carrying troops to Europe, not one troop ship was sunk by a U-boat.

Victory in Europe

In March 1918, the Germans began a new series of attacks all across Europe: The Germans hoped to defeat the British and French before American troops arrived to help the Allies.

At first, the German attacks were successful. In France, German forces pushed the Allies back nearly to Paris, the French capital. But by May, thousands of American troops had landed in France. Those troops helped the Allies stop the German advance 40 miles east of Paris.

In July, American and Allied troops began an attack of their own. By fall 1918, the Germans were retreating in all the war zones. Germany asked for peace.

On November 11, 1918, Germany signed an *armistice*. (An armistice is a simple agreement to stop fighting. It is not a peace treaty, which is worked out later.)

Americans were divided about the League of Nations. This political cartoon criticizes Congress for not acting to join the League.

The biggest war thus far had ended. Britain had lost nearly a million soldiers, France nearly a million and a half, and Germany nearly two million. About five million civilians had died of starvation and disease. All together, more than ten million people had died, including 116,000 Americans.

President Wilson's Peace Plan

In early 1918, months before the war ended, President Wilson had announced a plan that he believed would lead to a better, more peaceful world. The plan was called the **Fourteen Points**.

Some of the most important of President Wilson's Fourteen Points were:

- All nations should have freedom of the seas in both peace and war.
- All nations should reduce the size of their armed forces.
- People in all lands have the right to be independent and to decide what kind of government they will have.
- An "association of nations" should be set up to settle international disputes.

The association of nations became known as the **League of Nations**. To President Wilson, it was the most important part of his peace plan. Wilson believed the association would bring about the lasting peace he dreamed of.

Looking Back

1. How did the United States help the Allies defeat Germany?
2. What did President Wilson believe his peace plan would do?
3. What was the League of Nations?

The Treaty of Versailles Punishes Germany

In January 1919, leaders from 27 nations met to work out a peace treaty. The leaders met in Versailles, a town near Paris, France. President Wilson represented the United States at the peace conference.

Wilson urged other leaders to accept his Fourteen Points as the basis for the peace treaty. He also asked the leaders to treat all nations, including Germany, fairly in the treaty.

But many leaders objected to some of Wilson's Fourteen Points. And most of the leaders wanted to punish Germany for its part in the war. They also wanted to weaken Germany so that it could never again make war.

After months of discussion, the leaders agreed on a treaty. It was called the **Treaty of Versailles**. Some of President Wilson's ideas became part of the treaty, including his idea for the League of Nations.

But the treaty was harsher toward Germany than Wilson wanted: Germany was forced to accept the blame for starting the war. It lost part of its territory and all of its colonies. It was forced to pay $33 billion to the Allies for war damages. And Germany was forced to greatly reduce the size of its army and navy.

President Wilson feared that the treaty would cause bitterness in Germany—bitterness that might lead to future conflicts. But the President signed the treaty because it included his idea for the League of Nations.

The Senate Rejects the Treaty

In July 1919, President Wilson sent the treaty to the Senate for approval. (The Constitution says the Senate must approve all treaties.) Many members of the Senate opposed the treaty, mainly because of the League of Nations.

Senators who opposed the League of Nations were led by **Henry Cabot Lodge** of Massachusetts. Lodge pointed out that members of the League of Nations were called upon to help any other member nation that was attacked. Lodge argued that if the United States joined the League, it might become involved in future European wars. And Americans wanted no part of any future European conflicts.

Early in September 1919, President Wilson decided to speak directly to the American people about the League of Nations. He hoped to stir up so much support for the League that the Senate would have to approve the treaty.

President Wilson traveled the country by train. In town after town, he explained how important the League of Nations was to world peace. Wherever he traveled, large crowds turned out to hear the President. But the trip exhausted Wilson. On September 25, 1919, the President became seriously ill.

The President remained very ill for several months. He could not carry on his fight for the League. In March 1920, the Senate made its final rejection of the Treaty of Versailles. The United States did not become a member of the League of Nations.

Looking Back

1. What was Germany forced to do to meet the terms of the Treaty of Versailles?
2. Why did some senators oppose the League of Nations?

Chapter 21   **Review**

FOOD WILL
You came here seeking Free
You must now help to preser
WHEAT is needed for th
Waste nothin

Facts First

Use words below to complete each sentence.

alliances   Senate
industries   U-boats
League of Nations   war bonds
neutral   World War I

1. By 1914, many European nations had made _____ with other nations.
2. An assassination in Europe started _____.
3. At the start of the war, the United States was _____.
4. Attacks by German _____ helped bring the United States into the war.
5. In 1917, the government took control of many _____.
6. The government sold _____ to help pay for the war.
7. The Treaty of Versailles called for a _____ to settle disputes between countries.
8. The _____ rejected the Treaty of Versailles.

Word Check

Write the meaning of each of these words. Then use each word in a sentence.

draft   relations
markets   technology

Skill Builder

The government printed patriotic posters during World War I. Imagine what one of those posters must have been like. Then draw it. Use one of the titles below or make up your own title.

• Your Army Needs You
• Do Your Bit, Buy Bonds
• Food Is Ammunition, Don't Waste It
• Help the War, Plant a Victory Garden

Chapter 21 Notes

Read over the chapter. Find answers to these questions:

1. How did a war between Serbia and Austria-Hungary turn into a world war?
2. What actions taken by the German government led the United States to enter the war against Germany?
3. How did each of the following help organize the United States for war?
   a. the draft
   b. the War Industries Board
   c. the Food Administration
4. How did each of the following help support the United States war effort?
   a. war bonds
   b. the Committee on Public Information
   c. the Espionage Act
5. Why did the Senate reject the Treaty of Versailles?

Be a Historian

During World War I, American women were allowed to join the army for the first time. Interview a woman who is (or was) in the armed forces. Ask these questions:

1. Why did you join the armed forces?
2. What kind of training did you receive?
3. Do you think men and women are treated equally in the armed forces? Why do you say that?

Bonus

Today, American men must register for the draft when they reach the age of 18. Find out how they register. Call a post office or selective service office. Also find out who may be excused for religious reasons. Ask a priest, minister, or rabbi. Then report what you learned.

Unit 7  **Review**

What Do You Know?

Complete each sentence by choosing the correct ending.

1. Before the Civil War, the United States
   a. often became involved in Europe's affairs.
   b. usually stayed out of foreign affairs.
   c. built a huge empire in Latin America.

2. The United States began to expand into the Pacific when it
   a. bought Mexico.
   b. entered World War I.
   c. gained control of islands in the Pacific.

3. Victory in the Spanish-American War
   a. gave the United States control of Mexico.
   b. made the United States a world power.
   c. won Alaska for the United States.

4. In the Monroe Doctrine, President Monroe
   a. declared war on Germany.
   b. ordered Spain to free Cuba.
   c. warned European nations to stay out of the Americas.

5. America built the Panama Canal to connect
   a. the Atlantic and Pacific oceans.
   b. Lake Erie and the Hudson River.
   c. the Mississippi and Ohio rivers.

6. One cause of World War I was
   a. the Cuban revolution.
   b. the building of the Panama Canal.
   c. competition that led to alliances among European nations.

7. One reason the United States entered World War I was to
   a. protect the world's democracies.
   b. gain new territories in Europe.
   c. help Germany defeat the Allies.

What Do You Think?

Since World War I, the United States has become involved in other foreign wars throughout the world—in Europe, Asia, Africa, and Latin America. Some Americans believe that the United States should stay out of foreign wars entirely. What do you think?

Skill Builder

Find out in what years these events happened. Then write them in order.
- World War I begins in Europe.
- The Senate rejects the Treaty of Versailles.
- President James Monroe announces the Monroe Doctrine.
- The United States declares war on Germany.
- The warship *Maine* explodes in Cuba.
- America wins the Spanish-American War.

Unit 7 Notes

Look over the unit to find answers to these questions:
1. What is an imperialist nation?
2. What was the Spanish-American War?
3. What policies were set forth in the Monroe Doctrine and the Roosevelt Corollary?
4. Why was the Panama Canal built?
5. How did alliances result in World War I?
6. Why did the United States enter World War I?

Word Builder

Write a story about how America came to be a world power. Use all the key words listed below.

Key Words

isolate

neutral

policy

relations

world affairs

unit 8 Into Modern Times

May 20, 1932—somewhere over the Atlantic

In the dark night sky, a small plane is flying into a storm. Strong winds toss the plane about, and the pilot struggles to keep control of it. The pilot is Amelia Earhart, and she is all alone.

Earhart must make a difficult decision: Should she try to fly through the storm and risk crashing into the sea? Or should she turn back to North America? If she turns back, she will be giving up her dream of becoming the first woman to fly alone across the Atlantic.

Earhart has faced danger often since she learned to fly planes 12 years ago. She makes up her mind: She will go on. She flies on toward Europe, fighting to keep her bucking plane on course.

Earhart has no way of knowing how far above the ocean she is. She tries to climb out of the storm. But as she climbs, ice forms on the plane's wings.

Suddenly, she loses control. The plane goes into a spin. Earhart nearly crashes into the sea before she brings the plane back under control.

Finally, the storm is behind her. Night becomes morning. Earhart sees a welcome sight ahead—the green fields of Ireland. She has reached a country off the coast of Great Britain.

Earhart flies low over farms and lands her plane in a field. A farm worker runs out to the field and stares in amazement. Earhart smiles and says, ''I've come from America.''

In Our Time

When Amelia Earhart flew across the Atlantic, the United States was suffering from the worst depression in its history. Many Americans had no jobs and no homes. The American economy was in trouble.

Amelia Earhart was greatly admired by Americans during those troubled times. People like Earhart stood for American courage and determination. They showed that Americans had the ability to survive.

Today, the nation still admires Americans who show courage and determination. Who are some Americans that people admire today?

Warren Harding elected President		Herbert Hoover elected President		Franklin Roosevelt elected President		Pearl Harbor attacked by Japan	
1920	1924	1928	1929	1932	1939	1941	1945
	Calvin Coolidge becomes President		Stock Market crash		Start of World War II		Harry Truman becomes President End of World War II

Chapter 22 **The Years After the War**

Historical Pictures Service, Chicago

The 19th Amendment gave women the right to vote in 1920. Suffragette Alice Paul, *right*, casts the first vote.

During the years following World War I, the United States went through a period of great growth and change. Industries and technology grew rapidly. For many Americans, that growth meant better jobs, more money, and faster ways to get work done. Americans also now had time and money for entertainment.

Nearly every part of American life changed in the 1920s. Many historians see the 1920s as the beginning of ''modern times.'' During the 1920s, American life began to seem very much like it is today.

- Why did American industry grow during the years following World War I?
- How did Ford improve automobile production?
- How were Americans entertained?
- How did some groups of people suffer during the years after the war?

Key Words   You will be using these words in this chapter. Look them up in the glossary at the back of Part 2.

assemble	**prosperity**
productivity	**regulation**

Back to Normal

When World War I ended, Americans were eager for the nation to get back to normal. They were tired of the ways that government had controlled their lives. And they were tired of not being able to buy the things they wanted.

In 1920, the Republican Party nominated **Warren Harding** of Ohio for President. Harding's campaign slogan was ''Back to Normalcy.'' Harding said Americans should get back to the business of making a living and building the nation's economy. He also said that America should stay out of the affairs of other countries.

Most voters agreed with Harding; they voted for him by over seven million votes.

Corruption under President Harding

President Harding appointed many of his friends to important government offices. President Harding was honest, but many of those friends were not. Corruption became a problem during Harding's term of office.

President Harding became suddenly ill and died on August 2, 1923. Vice-President **Calvin Coolidge** then became President. President Coolidge forced corrupt officials to resign. He appointed honest people to take their places. His actions helped to restore people's trust in the government. In 1924, Coolidge ran for President. A large majority of Americans voted for him.

Looking Back

1. What did Warren Harding promise when he campaigned for President?
2. How did corrupt people become government officials under President Harding?

Library of Congress

These Model Ts came off the assembly line in the 1920s.

A New Prosperity for Americans

President Coolidge was a strong supporter of American business. He once said "the business of America is business." He meant that Americans had to work to keep America's businesses strong, because businesses brought **prosperity** to America.

Congress Supports Business

Most members of Congress were also supporters of business. Under Harding and Coolidge, Congress reduced the amount of taxes that corporations had to pay the government. Congress also passed laws to protect American businesses from foreign competition. Congress raised tariffs to their highest levels in history.

Regulation of Business Is Reduced

Years earlier, Congress had set up the **Interstate Commerce Commission (ICC)** and the **Federal Trade Commission (FTC)**. Those were government offices that were supposed to regulate business and trade.

But President Coolidge believed that government should leave business alone. He appointed people who supported business to the FTC and ICC. They made sure that government **regulation** of business was as limited as possible.

More Jobs and Increased Productivity

The 1920s were a period of tremendous growth for business. One reason for the growth was that many new kinds of industries developed. Another reason was the rise in **productivity**—the amount of goods that factories produce. Between 1921 and 1929, the amount of goods produced by American factories nearly doubled. Exports nearly tripled.

Business people increased productivity by using new electric-powered machines that could produce goods more quickly than old methods. Business leaders also hired *efficiency experts*. Those experts suggested ways to help workers do their jobs more quickly.

New businesses and industries and increased productivity meant many new jobs for Americans. For many families, the 1920s were good years.

Not Everyone Shares in the Good Times

Not all Americans were *prosperous* (doing well). Blacks, Native Americans, Mexicans, Asians, and other *minority groups* could get only low-paying, unskilled jobs.

Workers in some industries also were not doing well. For example, many workers in the coal and textile industries were unemployed.

Farmers were also having hard times. During the war, crop prices had gone up. Many farmers had borrowed money to buy land and farm machinery. After the war, crop prices fell. Many farmers lost their farms because they could not make enough money to pay off their debts.

Looking Back
1. How did Congress support business?
2. How did businesses increase their productivity?

The Automobile Industry

One of the most important industries of the 1920s was the automobile industry. American businesses had been making automobiles since the 1890s. At that time, automobiles were expensive to make, and only wealthy people could afford them.

In 1903, businessman **Henry Ford** set up the Ford Motor Company. He wanted to make an inexpensive car that most Americans could afford. In 1908, he designed a car called the Model T. It cost $950 to buy. For most people, the price was still too high.

Ford Improves Automobile Production

In 1914, Ford brought the cost of the Model T down by finding a faster way to *assemble* cars. He set up an **assembly line** that used electric machines.

An assembly line is a team of workers who assemble a product. Each worker adds just one part of the product, then passes it on to the next worker. That worker then adds another part, and passes the product on to other workers.

Ford's assembly line worked like this: The frame of a car was built at one end of the factory. The frame was then attached to a moving machine that pulled it in a straight *line* through the factory. Workers stood at work stations along the line. As the frame of the car moved past, each worker, using electric-powered machinery, added one part of the car. By the time the car reached the end of the line, it was completely put together.

With the assembly line, workers cut the time needed to manufacture a Model T from 14 hours to 90 minutes. The cost of the Model T also went down. By 1924, Ford was selling Model Ts for $260. At that price, Ford could sell over a million cars a year.

This U.S. postage stamp honors the automobile industry.

Other manufacturers copied Ford's methods and made cars that many Americans could afford to buy. By 1929, there were over 23 million cars in the United States.

The Auto Industry Helps Other Industries Grow

The growth of the automobile industry led to the growth of other industries and businesses. For example, automobile factories needed large amounts of steel and glass for their cars. So, the steel and glass industries grew. Factories needed rubber for car tires, so the rubber industry grew. Cars used gasoline as fuel. That led to a boom in the oil industry. (Gasoline is refined from oil.)

Now that millions of Americans owned cars, those Americans wanted better roads. State governments hired companies to pave dirt roads and build new highways. That meant more business for concrete and asphalt companies.

The tourist industry also grew because of the automobile. Many Americans used their cars to travel around the country. Restaurants, gasoline stations, and automobile repair businesses opened to meet the tourists' needs.

By 1930, one out of every nine Americans held a job that was connected in some way to the automobile industry.

Looking Back

1. How did Henry Ford improve automobile production?
2. How does an assembly line work?
3. What other industries were helped by the growth of the automobile industry?

Famous entertainers of the 1920s
were (*left to right*) singer Enrico Caruso,
Helen Wills, Babe Ruth, and movie star Rudolph Valentino.

This family listens to an early radio program.

The Entertainment Industry Grows

In the 1920s, many American workers were earning more money than ever before. They were also working fewer hours. Americans had more *leisure time*—time to spend as they wanted. They also had more money to spend on entertainment.

New industries grew up to entertain people. In the past, Americans had usually made up their own entertainment. They also saw plays, circuses, and traveling shows that came to their towns and cities. In the 1920s, new forms of *mass entertainment* developed. That was entertainment that reached millions of people.

Motion Pictures

Making motion pictures became a big business during the 1920s. Motion pictures had been invented in the 1880s. In the early 1900s, they became popular. By the 1920s, Hollywood had become the center of the motion picture industry. The movies were in black and white, and they had no sound.

Then, in 1927, the first "talking picture" appeared. That movie was called *The Jazz Singer*. Millions of Americans poured into movie theaters to see—and hear—*The Jazz Singer*. The movie's great success led to the making of more talking pictures.

Radio

Radios stations had been broadcasting in America since 1915. In 1920, WWJ in Detroit and KDKA in Pittsburgh became the first *commercial radio stations*. A commercial radio station makes money by selling an advertising service: Businesses pay it to tell listeners about their products.

By 1929, radio had become an industry. Over 700 commercial radio stations in the United States were broadcasting news, music, and comedy programs into millions of homes.

Sports

Sports grew in popularity during the 1920s. Baseball players such as **Babe Ruth** and **Ty Cobb** became national heroes. Women also became famous. Tennis player **Helen Wills** won dozens of championships in the 1920s. In 1926, **Gertrude Ederle** became the first woman to swim across the *English Channel*, between England and France. Until then, only men had done that. Ederle broke the men's record by about 2 hours.

The most famous record was set by **Charles Lindbergh**. In 1927, he made the first solo airplane flight across the Atlantic Ocean. One hundred thousand people greeted him when he landed in Paris, France.

Looking Back

1. Why did many Americans have more money and leisure time in the 1920s?
2. How did Americans spend their leisure time?
3. Why do you think mass entertainment became big business at this time?

Civil Rights: Not Equal for All

The years after the war seemed good for America. The country was at peace, industry grew, and people found new ways to have fun. But many Americans still struggled to gain their full rights as citizens.

Women Gain the Vote

In 1920, after 72 years of struggle, the women's suffrage movement finally gained its goal. Women won the right to vote throughout the nation.

Congress approved the **Nineteenth Amendment** to the Constitution in 1919. That amendment said that no citizen can be kept from voting "on account of sex." In 1920, the Nineteenth Amendment was ratified and added to the Constitution.

Women's lives changed in other ways at that time. Women began to demand a new freedom of living after 1920. They wore shorter hair and shorter skirts. And more women began to work outside the home. But women were refused many jobs and paid less than men.

Blacks Face Prejudice

World War I had created many new job opportunities in wartime industry. Many Blacks moved north to fill those jobs. Black soldiers returning from the war also expected to find jobs in northern industry. Instead, Blacks arriving in the North found there were not enough jobs to go around. And White workers feared losing their jobs to the Blacks.

Conflicts developed between Blacks and Whites. When Blacks looked for jobs or moved into "White" neighborhoods, they were sometimes attacked. In several cities, riots broke out between the races. Mobs of Whites and Blacks fought each other, and people were killed.

Native Americans Live in Poverty

In the 1800s, Native Americans were forced to move to reservations. The government promised Native Americans that reservation lands would always belong to them. Then Congress passed the Dawes Act in 1887. That Act split up reservation lands. Much of that land was sold to Whites.

When the reservations were split up, tribes of Native Americans were also split up. Many Native Americans lost contact with their *culture* (traditions and values). And altogether, Native Americans also lost over 60 percent of the land they had owned. They lived in poverty.

The Native American population began to get smaller. Native Americans came to be called the "vanishing Americans."

In 1924, Congress passed the **Indian Citizenship Act**. All Native Americans born in the territory of the United States became citizens.

In many states, however, Native Americans still could not vote. And two years after the Citizenship Act, a study showed that most American Indians were still living in poverty—in poor health and with poor education.

Looking Back

1. What does the Nineteenth Amendment say?
2. What problem did women face when looking for jobs in the 1920s?
3. Why did many Blacks move to the North during and after the war?
4. Why were there race riots in the North after the war?
5. How did the Dawes Act make life more difficult for Native Americans?

Chapter 22

Review

Facts First

Use words below to complete each sentence.

assembly line   **productivity**
business   **radio**
corruption   **tariffs**
leisure time   **vote**

1. During President Harding's term, _____ in government was a serious problem.
2. President Coolidge strongly supported _____.
3. Congress raised _____ to protect businesses from foreign competition.
4. Factories increased _____ by using machines powered by electricity.
5. Ford increased automobile production by using an _____.
6. Shorter working hours meant more _____ for workers.
7. Americans turned to _____ and motion pictures for entertainment.
8. In 1920, the Nineteenth Amendment gave women the right to _____.

Word Check

Write the meaning of each of these words. Then use each word in a sentence.

> **assemble**   **prosperity**
> **productivity**   **regulation**

Skill Builder

Many American writers, musicians, and other artists of the 1920s are still remembered today for their work. Find out about one of these artists. Then report what you learned.

Louis Armstrong   George Gershwin
Mary Cassatt   Ernest Hemingway
Willa Cather   Langston Hughes
F. Scott Fitzgerald   Bessie Smith
Robert Frost   Gertrude Stein

Chapter 22 Notes

Read over the chapter. Find answers to these questions:

1. How did both electric-powered machines and efficiency experts help industries increase their productivity?
2. What new method of production did Henry Ford use in order to produce an inexpensive car?
3. How did the growth of the automobile industry help other industries grow as well?
4. How did life change for American women in the 1920s?
5. How was life difficult for Blacks and for Native Americans in the 1920s?

Be a Historian

Find out how Americans these days spend their free time. Conduct a survey. Ask friends, classmates, and neighbors this question: What do you enjoy doing most in your free time?

Bonus

1. A new kind of music became popular in America in the 1920s—jazz. Bring in tapes or records of jazz music from the 1920s.
2. In 1919, the Eighteenth Amendment was added to the Constitution. That amendment *prohibited* (banned) the making, selling, or buying of alcohol. As a result, the 1920s are sometimes called the "Age of Prohibition." Find out more about Prohibition. Then report what you learned.

Chapter 23 The Great Depression

Library of Congress

A soup kitchen provides free food to these men looking for work during the depression.

In 1928, President Coolidge did not run for re-election, and the Republican Party chose Herbert Hoover to run for President. During his campaign, Hoover told Americans that the economy was strong and would grow even stronger.

Just a year later, the nation entered the worst depression in its history. In 1932, Democrat Franklin Roosevelt was elected President. Under President Roosevelt, Congress passed hundreds of laws to deal with the depression. The federal government began to play a greater role in the everyday lives of millions of Americans.

- How did the depression begin?
- How were Americans affected by the depression?
- How did President Roosevelt and Congress deal with the depression?
- How did the relationship between government and the people change during the depression?

Key Words   You will be using these words in this chapter. Look them up in the glossary at the back of Part 2.

minimum wage   **unemployment**
stock market   **welfare**

The Boom Slows Down

When President Hoover took office in 1929, the American economy seemed to be booming still. But America was beginning to have trouble with its economy.

One problem was *overproduction*—producing more goods than people could buy. As you read in Chapter 22, businesses greatly increased their productivity in the 1920s. Many began to produce far more goods than needed. So, businesses laid off workers. Those unemployed workers and their families then had less money to spend. Less goods were bought and sales fell off. Businesses then laid off even more people.

Another problem was in America's rural areas. A few years earlier, the economy had been booming for farmers and rural business people. World War I was being fought, and there was a great demand for American food in Europe. Farmers sold their products for high prices. But after the war, European farmers were able to farm again. The demand for American food decreased. Prices fell, and many American farmers could not make enough money. They could not afford to buy goods, and business in rural areas suffered.

Looking Back
1. How did overproduction cause problems in the economy?
2. Why did business in rural areas suffer after World War I?

Left: These shacks were homes for unemployed people in Seattle, Washington. This village was called "Hooverville." *Above:* These men in New York City lived in a shack in an empty lot. They spent their days looking for jobs.

AP/Wide World Photos

The Stock Market Crash

In the 1920s, many people bought stock in companies. If a company makes a good profit, the price of its stock goes up. Stockholders can then sell their stock at a higher price than they paid to buy it. In that way, those stockholders can make a profit.

During the 1920s, most companies were profitable. Stock prices rose steadily. For example, the price of stock in Radio Corporation of America rose 600 percent between 1928 and 1929. Stockholders who sold their stock made six times the amount they paid for it.

Newspapers in the 1920s carried stories of people who made huge fortunes by *investing* in (putting money into) stocks. More and more Americans hoped to "get rich quick" by investing in stocks. People spent their life savings or borrowed money to buy stock.

As more Americans bought stock, stock prices went up. Americans were sure stock prices would continue to rise. Few people thought about what would happen if prices went down.

Falling Stock Prices Cause a Crash

By September 1929, prices of stock had risen to record heights on the **New York Stock Exchange**. A stock exchange is a place where people buy and sell stock. The largest stock exchange was (and still is) in New York City.

In October, prices began to fall. Worried stockholders began selling their stocks. Because of that, prices of stock fell even lower. As more stockholders sold their stocks, the prices fell lower and lower.

Then, on October 29, the *stock market crashed*. That meant prices dropped rapidly in one day. People panicked. They tried to sell their stocks at any price, but there were few buyers.

The stock market crash ruined many Americans: Wealthy people who had invested millions in stocks were suddenly poor. Many Americans lost their life savings.

Looking Back

1. Why did many people invest in stocks in the 1920s?
2. Why did people suddenly start selling their stocks in October 1929?
3. What happened to the prices of stock when the stock market *crashed*?

The Depression Begins

The stock market crash began the longest depression in the nation's history. It lasted over ten years. The depression was so damaging that it came to be called the **Great Depression**.

Banks Fail

As soon as the stock market crashed, many banks began to fail.

A bank needs a certain amount of money in order to do business. It gets that amount from the money that people *deposit* (put) into bank accounts. The bank uses the deposited money to make loans to people and businesses.

In the 1920s, many banks loaned money for stock investments. When the stock market crashed, those loans were not repaid. Banks that lost most of their money had to close their doors and go out of business.

All across the nation, people rushed to their banks to try to take out their money. But many of the banks were closed. Banks that were still open were left with no money after people removed their deposits. Then those banks had to close also. Between 1930 and 1932, nearly 5000 banks failed. Most people who had accounts in those banks lost all their money.

Unemployment Rises

By 1932, nearly one American worker in four was out of a job. People walked the streets looking for work. But they could find no jobs anywhere.

Some groups suffered more than others. Black and Mexican workers were often the first to be fired. And married women had a hard time finding jobs. Some states passed laws against hiring them for government jobs.

Hunger and Homelessness

Many families lost their homes when they ran out of money. Some people built shacks out of scrap wood in vacant lots. Thousands of people left their hometowns to look for jobs. But no one was hiring.

In 1932, newspapers began reporting that people were starving. In cities, people searched garbage cans for food. *Soup kitchens* served free food to the hungry.

Yet, there was plenty of food in America. Farm prices were so low that farmers did not bother to pick crops or sell milk and meat. Food rotted in the fields.

The Federal Government Acts

At first, President Hoover believed that businesses would solve their problems and bring the country out of the depression.

But the depression became worse. In 1930, Hoover asked Congress to spend money on *public works*. Those were government projects, such as building highways and dams. Such projects created jobs.

In 1932, Congress set up the **Reconstruction Finance Corporation** (**RFC**) to help businesses that were failing. The RFC loaned money to banks, railroads, and insurance companies. RFC loans helped some businesses, but thousands of others closed during 1932.

By then, many Americans blamed Hoover for the hard times. Groups of shacks built by the homeless were called "Hoovervilles." Empty pockets turned inside out were known as "Hoover flags."

Looking Back
1. Why did banks fail?
2. How did the depression affect Americans?
3. How did the federal government provide relief for businesses in 1932?

Programs such as the WPA provided jobs for the unemployed. Hoover Dam, *left*, was built and the mural at Coit Tower in San Francisco, *right*, was painted under such programs.

Bureau of Reclamation

Artist: Maxine Albro, California Agriculture 1934, PWAP, Coit Tower, San Francisco. Photographer: Don Beatty © 1981

The New Deal

The year of 1932 was an election year. The Republican Party nominated President Hoover for re-election. The Democratic Party nominated **Franklin Roosevelt**, the governor of New York.

During the campaign, Roosevelt promised "a new deal for the American people." He meant that under his leadership, the government would make laws that could end the depression and help the needy.

Voters chose Roosevelt over Hoover by more than seven million votes.

Roosevelt Takes Action

President Roosevelt took office in March 1933. (Up until 1937, all United States Presidents took office on March 4. **Amendment 20** made January 20 the day that the President's term begins and ends.) President Roosevelt immediately began to put into action a plan that he and his advisors had developed to end the depression. That plan became known as the **New Deal**.

In those years, Congress always began its session a few weeks after a new President began his term. President Roosevelt called a special session of Congress to start earlier. During the next three months, the President sent 15 bills concerning the depression to Congress. Congress approved each law.

Government Helps the Banks

One of President Roosevelt's first actions was to close all the nation's banks. Congress then passed the **Emergency Banking Relief Act**. The Act allowed banks to reopen only if they could prove to the government that they were *sound*, or in no danger of failing.

Then President Roosevelt spoke to Americans on the radio. It was the first in a series of talks that Roosevelt called "fireside chats." President Roosevelt guaranteed Americans that their money would be safe in the reopened banks. The President's confidence and strong, steady voice soothed Americans' fears. Within a few weeks, the banking crisis passed.

Help for the Needy

President Roosevelt had three goals in his New Deal plan:

- to provide relief to needy Americans and find jobs for the unemployed;
- to bring about an economic *recovery*, or return to normal, by helping business and agriculture; and
- to reform the nation's economy so depressions would not develop again.

Congress moved quickly to help the President reach the first of his goals—help for the needy. In May 1933, Congress set up the **Federal Emergency Relief Administration (FERA)**. FERA provided money for needy Americans to pay for food and clothing. By 1935, FERA had spent over two billion dollars in aid to the needy.

Help for the Unemployed

Congress also acted quickly to provide jobs for the unemployed. Government leaders believed that jobs would provide workers with money to spend. If more people spent money, the economy would improve.

In 1933, Congress set up the **Civilian Conservation Corps** (**CCC**). The CCC put young men to work on *conservation* projects. The conservation projects helped preserve and protect natural resources such as forests, rivers, and wild life. CCC workers planted trees, dug reservoirs, and fought forest fires.

In 1935, Congress set up the **Works Progress Administration** (**WPA**). WPA workers built hospitals, airports, schools, and roads. WPA actors, musicians, and singers performed around the country. By 1936, about four million people were working for the WPA.

Helping Farmers Recover

Congress also acted quickly to help President Roosevelt reach his second goal—economic recovery. Congress first helped farmers. In 1933, Congress set up the **Agricultural Adjustment Administration** (**AAA**).

You read that farmers suffered even before the depression because of low food prices. During the depression, farm prices remained low mainly because farmers were producing more food than people could buy.

In 1933, the government began to pay farmers *not* to grow certain crops, such as wheat, rice, and sugar. In that way, the prices of those crops would rise. By 1935, prices of farm products had risen sharply.

Helping Business Recover

During the early years of the depression, many businesses were in trouble. Business people cut prices. Competition became unfair. That resulted in business failures and **unemployment**.

To help business, Congress set up the **National Recovery Administration** (**NRA**). The NRA encouraged businesses to work together to set fair prices and end unfair competition. Leaders from different industries, such as the automobile industry and the textile industry, met to set up *codes*, or rules. The codes described how much a company could produce and how much it could charge for its products.

At first, many businesses cooperated with the NRA. But by 1934, companies stopped following the NRA codes.

The Supreme Court Attacks the New Deal

President Roosevelt believed the federal government had to expand its power to deal with an emergency like the depression. But some Americans believed that certain New Deal laws, such as the laws that set up the NRA and AAA, were unconstitutional: Some people believed those laws gave the federal government more power than it was allowed under the Constitution.

In 1935, the Supreme Court declared the NRA unconstitutional. In 1936, the Court declared the AAA unconstitutional. In both cases, the Court said the federal government had gone beyond its powers under the Constitution.

Looking Back
1. What was the New Deal?
2. What were President Roosevelt's goals for the New Deal?
3. How did the New Deal help the jobless?
4. Why did the Supreme Court find some New Deal laws unconstitutional?

New Deal Reforms

During the New Deal years, Congress passed several laws to correct problems in the economy that had led to the depression.

For example, Congress passed the **Truth-in-Securities Act** to control the stock market. The Act set up the **Securities and Exchange Commission (SEC)**. The SEC watches over the stock market and regulates the buying and selling of stock.

Congress also reformed the nation's banking system. The **Glass-Steagall Banking Act** was passed to protect Americans from bank failures. It also set up the **Federal Deposit Insurance Corporation (FDIC)**. The FDIC *insures*, or protects from loss, people's savings. If a bank fails, the FDIC pays its depositors the full amount of their savings. The FDIC continues to insure people's savings today.

Other Reforms Help Workers

Other New Deal reforms helped workers. During the depression, many companies tried to keep workers from joining unions. In 1935, Congress passed the **National Labor Relations Act**. The Act guaranteed workers the right to join a union.

Many companies forced workers to work longer hours during the depression. At the same time, wages were cut. In 1938, Congress passed the **Fair Labor Standards Act**. The Act set the *maximum*, or longest, work week at 44 hours. The Act said that businesses must pay extra to workers who work more than 44 hours.

The Act also set a ***minimum wage*** of 25 cents an hour. (Since 1938, the minimum wage has been raised many times.) The Act also prohibited the hiring of children under 16 to work in factories.

Social Security

In 1935, Congress passed the **Social Security Act** to help the aged, unemployed, and disabled. The Act was the first national *welfare* law in history.

The Social Security Act set up a plan for paying *pensions* to people over 65. (A pension is money paid to people who no longer work.) The Act also helped the states set up unemployment insurance plans that give unemployed people money to live on while they look for work.

The Act also provided money for states to help homeless children, and the blind and other disabled people.

The Importance of the New Deal

The New Deal brought some lasting changes to American life. Before the New Deal, most Americans had little contact with the federal government. But during the New Deal, federal programs brought government into the lives of nearly every American. Millions of Americans worked for the government or received government *benefits*—money or other aid. They still do today.

Before the New Deal, most Americans believed that the government should not interfere with the economy. Today, most Americans expect the government to do what it can to keep the economy healthy.

Many New Deal reforms, such as social security, the maximum work week, the minimum wage, and restrictions on child labor, have lasted. They continue to protect workers and improve lives today.

Looking Back
1. How did Congress reform the stock market and the nation's banks?
2. How did New Deal reforms help workers?
3. What did the Social Security Act do?
4. What lasting changes did the New Deal bring to American life?

Chapter 23

Review

Facts First

Use words below to complete each sentence.

businesses	**laws**
depression	**New Deal**
Franklin Roosevelt	**regulate**
Herbert Hoover	**social security**
jobs	**stock market**

1. Problems in the economy of the 1920s led to a _____.
2. The depression began when the _____ crashed.
3. Thousands of banks and _____ closed during the depression.
4. Millions of Americans lost their _____ and homes during the depression.
5. President _____ did not believe the government should interfere with business.
6. _____ defeated Herbert Hoover in the election of 1932.
7. The _____ was President Roosevelt's program for dealing with the depression.
8. Congress passed 15 _____ to deal with the depression right after Roosevelt took office.
9. To _____ the stock market, Congress set up the Securities and Exchange Commission.
10. Congress set up the _____ system to aid older Americans, the jobless, and the needy.

Word Check

Write the meanings of these words. Then use them in sentences.

minimum wage	**unemployment**
stock market	**welfare**

Skill Builder

The social security program helps millions of Americans. Find out about the program by calling or visiting a Social Security Administration office. Or check a library for information on social security. Then answer these questions:

1. What kinds of help does the social security program give people?
2. Who pays for social security?
3. How does someone get a social security card?

Chapter 23 Notes

Read over the chapter. Find answers to these questions:

1. What happened to stock prices during the stock market crash of 1929? Why?
2. How did Americans' lives change because of the depression?
3. How did New Deal administrations help workers, farmers, and businesses during the depression?
4. Why were some New Deal laws declared unconstitutional by the Supreme Court?
5. How are some New Deal laws still protecting Americans today?

Bonus

Some remarkable women helped make the New Deal work. Find out about one of those women listed below. Then report what you learned.

Mary McLeod Bethune	Frances Perkins
Mary Dewson	Eleanor Roosevelt

Chapter 24 The Second World War (1939-1945)

Joe Rosenthal Photograph, Library of Congress

The famous photograph, *left,* shows U.S. troops raising the American flag after winning the Battle of Iwo Jima. The U.S. postage stamp honors the event.

At the end of World War I, most governments in Europe became republics with elected legislatures. Political parties fought to gain power. Most countries went through difficult economic times. The war had destroyed farms, towns, and cities all over Europe. People could not find work, food, or supplies they needed. By the 1930s, all of Europe was suffering from the Great Depression.

In Asia, countries were also affected by the Great Depression. They, too, were experiencing economic and political troubles.

In 1939, war broke out in Europe. In 1941, the United States was attacked. Americans were once again in a world war.

- How did the Second World War begin?
- Why did the United States enter the war?
- How did the United States prepare for war?
- How did the United States bring the war to an end?

Key Words You will be using these words in this chapter. Look them up in the glossary at the back of Part 2.

aggression	ration
dictator	totalitarian

Trouble in Europe and Asia

The Second World War was caused by three nations—Germany, Italy, and Japan. They had been taken over by *dictators* who set up *totalitarian* governments. The dictators came into power because of economic and political problems that developed after World War I.

Mussolini Takes Over Italy

In Italy, economic and political problems led to violent strikes and riots. **Benito Mussolini** was the leader of the Italian **Fascist Party**. He promised to end Italy's problems and bring order to the country. He also promised to make Italy a world power.

In 1922, Mussolini became Italy's premier. People who opposed him were threatened, beaten, and murdered. Soon, Mussolini had become dictator of Italy.

Hitler Takes Over Germany

In Germany, people were angry about the depression and high unemployment in their country. They were also angry about the peace treaties their leaders had signed after the war. The treaties punished Germany for the war. Germany had to pay huge war fines. It had to give up resources such as land and overseas colonies. It could not build up an army or keep troops in the *Rhineland*. (That was the strip of German land that bordered France.)

Adolph Hitler was the leader of the **Nazi Party**. He promised to end the depression in Germany and bring prosperity back to the country. He also promised to get back German territory and to rebuild Germany as a powerful world empire.

In 1933, Hitler became *chancellor*, or prime minister, of Germany. Like Mussolini, he used violence to crush people who opposed him. By 1934, Hitler was dictator. He set up a totalitarian government that controlled industries, schools, newspapers, and the police and military. He began to build up a powerful army.

Hitler gained support by telling the Germans that they belonged to a "master race." He said that the "master race" would rule the world. He also told Germans that Germany's problems were caused by Jews. He and his followers began a program of arresting, torturing, and murdering German Jews and other people that Hitler said were inferior and, therefore, enemies of Germany. Those included Gypsies, Slavs, and sick or disabled people.

A Military Power Grows in Asia

While Germany and Italy were building their military forces in Europe, Japan was becoming the strongest military power in Asia.

During the 1920s, Japan's military leaders began to take over the country. They used terrorism and violence to gain power. By 1937, military leaders had total control of the government. They set up a military dictatorship to rule the country.

Japan Begins Aggression

The dictators of Germany, Italy, and Japan wanted to expand their territories. They planned to do that through military *aggression*—invading other countries.

Japan was the first to act. In 1931, Japanese troops invaded northern China and seized Manchuria, which belonged to China. The League of Nations protested the invasion of China. But it did nothing to stop Japan.

Italy and Germany Act Next

In 1935, Italian troops invaded Ethiopia, a country in East Africa. They next invaded Albania, a country in Europe. The League of Nations and the United States protested Italy's actions but did nothing to stop Italy.

In 1936, Hitler sent German troops into the Rhineland. Britain and France protested that Germany was violating its peace treaties. But they did nothing to stop Germany.

War Begins

Next to Germany were the countries of Austria, Czechoslovakia, and Poland. In 1938, Germany invaded Austria.

Hitler then turned to Czechoslovakia. He demanded that part of it be placed under German control.

British and French leaders met with Hitler at a conference in Munich, Germany. At the **Munich Conference**, they agreed that Germany would control part of Czechoslovakia. In return, Hitler promised that Germany would seize no more territory.

But Hitler did not intend to honor the agreement. In March 1939, German troops took over all of Czechoslovakia. Then, on September 1, 1939, Germany attacked Poland without warning. On September 3, Britain and France declared war on Germany.

World War II had begun.

Looking Back

1. What did Mussolini and Hitler promise to do for their countries?
2. How did the League of Nations act when Japan, Italy, and Germany invaded other countries?
3. What agreement was made at the Munich Conference? Did Hitler honor the agreement?

The United States Enters the War

During World War II, Italy, Germany, and Japan formed an alliance. The alliance was called the *Rome-Berlin-Tokyo Axis*. The three countries became known as the **Axis Powers**, or the **Axis**. Britain and France and the countries that sided with them were called the **Allies**.

The Allies were not prepared for war in 1939. But the Axis had been building military power for years. Germany had a huge, well-trained army, equipped with the most modern tanks and other weapons. It also had the largest air force in the world.

Germany used a new form of warfare called *blitzkrieg* to quickly conquer most of western Europe. (*Blitzkrieg* is a German word meaning "lightning war.") Squadrons of German planes would suddenly appear to bomb a country's military bases and factories. At the same time, hundreds of German tanks and thousands of troops would quickly move into that country's cities. Using those methods, Germany conquered Poland and France, each within a month. Within three months, Germany had also conquered Denmark, Norway, the Netherlands, and Belgium.

Americans Support the Allies

In 1939, President Roosevelt declared that the United States would remain neutral in the war. But the President and most Americans supported the Allies: Americans believed that Germany and Italy were threats to democracies such as the United States. America began selling military supplies to the Allies. In 1940, President Roosevelt turned over 50 American warships to Britain.

By June 1940, Britain stood alone against Germany in Europe. During 1940 and 1941, German planes bombed British cities every night.

By late 1940, Britain was running out of money to buy American supplies. In 1941, Congress passed the **Lend-Lease Act**. The Act allowed the President to lend or *lease* (rent) war materials to Britain and the other Allies. Payment or return of the materials would be worked out after the war.

Getting materials to Britain was difficult. German submarines sank many British supply ships. In 1941, President Roosevelt ordered the American navy to escort British ships as far as Iceland. German submarines began to attack American ships.

Japan Attacks Hawaii

After Germany invaded France in 1940, Japan set up military bases in *French Indochina*, colonies in Southeast Asia that belonged to France. To show that it disapproved of that action, the United States stopped the sale of gasoline and many other items to Japan. America also made a large loan to China, to help China in its fight against the Japanese invasion.

On December 7, 1941, Japanese bombers attacked **Pearl Harbor**, an important naval base in Hawaii. The Japanese also attacked nearby air force bases. The attack caught Americans by surprise. In two hours, about 18 American ships and over 150 American planes were damaged or destroyed.

The next day, Congress declared war against Japan. Germany and Italy then declared war against the United States.

Looking Back
1. What were the Axis Powers?
2. How did the United States help Britain during the first years of the war?
3. Why did the United States declare war against Japan in 1941?

Left: During World War II, women did many jobs to help win the war. This picture shows a civilian pilot who instructed other women.
Right: Manzanar was a Japanese-American relocation camp in California. This photograph was taken by Ansel Adams, a famous photographer.

AP/Wide World Photos

Ansel Adams Photograph, Library of Congress

Americans at War

The attack on Pearl Harbor outraged Americans. Within weeks, thousands of Americans volunteered for the armed forces. By the end of the war, six million men and women had volunteered. Another ten million men were drafted.

The Government Rations Goods

The government declared that certain materials, such as rubber, gasoline, meat, and sugar were *essential*, or necessary, to the war effort. Those goods were needed by the armed forces.

The government began to **ration** essential goods. American families were given *ration stamps*, or coupons. Those stamps allowed people to buy only a certain amount of each rationed item.

American Production Increases

When the war began, many Americans were still unemployed because of the depression. But many jobs opened up during the war years and the depression ended.

In 1942, President Roosevelt set up the **War Production Board**. The board ordered factories to *convert* (change) from peacetime to wartime production. Automobile factories began to produce jeeps and tanks. Clothing companies began to produce uniforms. Other factories began to produce planes, ships, and other military supplies.

By 1944, American war production was twice that of Germany, Italy, and Japan combined. America's industrial output was an important reason that the Allies won the war.

The Japanese Relocation Camps

After Pearl Harbor was attacked, Japanese troops invaded country after country in Southeast Asia. In the United States, frightened Americans heard that California would be invaded next. They also heard stories about Japanese-American spies. The stories were not true. But in 1942, President Roosevelt ordered the army to *relocate* (move) 110,000 Japanese Americans from their homes on the west coast.

Men, women, and children were forced to give up their properties and live in huge camps surrounded by barbed-wire fences. Those camps were located in such places as the deserts of the West and Southwest. Armed soldiers kept watch over the Japanese Americans and made sure they did not leave. Japanese Americans were kept in such relocation camps until 1945.

Despite such treatment, many young Japanese Americans still wanted to fight for their country. In 1943, the **442nd Regimental Combat Team** was formed. It was an army unit that was made up almost entirely of Japanese-American soldiers.

The 442nd unit fought in Europe. It won more medals than any other unit its size.

Looking Back

1. How did the government organize industry to prepare for war?
2. What happened to Japanese Americans on the west coast after the attack on Pearl Harbor?
3. What was the 442nd Regimental Combat Team?

Main Axis nations
Under Axis control
Allied territory
Neutral countries

The War in Europe

Twenty-six nations had joined the Allies by 1942. (Later, the Allies would grow to include 49 nations.) The most powerful Allied nations were the United States, Britain, and the *Soviet Union* (Russia).

In January 1942, President Roosevelt and British Prime Minister **Winston Churchill** worked out the Allies' plan for winning the war: The Allies would first defeat Germany and Italy. Then they would defeat the Japanese in Asia.

Germany Advances in Russia and Africa

In June 1941, Germany had attacked the Soviet Union. By winter, German troops had advanced far into Soviet territory and were threatening the Soviet capital of Moscow.

German forces had also won control of much of North Africa. By summer 1942, German troops had pushed into Egypt and were trying to take the **Suez Canal** there.

The Suez Canal had been built by the French and was now under British-French control. It connected the Mediterranean Sea and the Red Sea. If Germany took the Suez Canal, the Germans would control the Mediterranean. They could then move easily into oil-rich Iran and Iraq.

The Allies Attack

In late 1942, the British defeated the Germans at El Alamein in Egypt, near the Suez Canal. The British then pushed the Germans west, across Egypt and Libya.

Meanwhile, American troops landed in Morocco and Algeria. The Americans then moved east across Algeria toward the British army in Egypt and Libya. The Germans were trapped between the two Allied armies. In May 1943, the Germans surrendered in Tunisia.

The Allied forces then moved north from Tunisia, invaded Sicily, and entered Italy. Members of Mussolini's government rebelled against him. They arrested Mussolini and put him into prison. (Mussolini escaped but was later captured and executed by the Italians.) In 1943, the Italian government surrendered to the Allies.

Soviet Forces Push the Germans Back

In the winter of 1941–1942, Soviet troops stopped the German advance on Moscow. Hitler then ordered German troops to capture Stalingrad in southern Russia. After months of bitter fighting, Soviet forces defeated the Germans there.

By 1944, Soviet forces had driven the Germans from the Soviet Union. Soviet troops also captured Romania, Bulgaria, and Hungary. Those were countries in eastern Europe that Germany had conquered.

Looking Back

1. What was the Allied plan for defeating the Axis?
2. Why was it important for the Allies to keep Germany from controlling the Suez Canal?
3. What did the Italian government do after putting Mussolini into prison in 1943?

Library of Congress

General George Patton was the commander of a U.S. tank division that helped win the war in Europe.

Allied Victory in Europe

Since early 1944, the Allies had been building a huge force in England. Tons of supplies and thousands of men were sent from America to England. The Allies planned to invade Europe, free France, and then invade Germany. General **Dwight Eisenhower** was in charge of the invasion. He was the commander of Allied forces in Europe. General Eisenhower picked June 6, 1944, as the invasion day. That day became known as **D-Day**.

The Invasion Begins

On June 6, thousands of ships and airplanes left England and crossed the English Channel to France. More than 120 thousand Allied soldiers landed on the beaches of Normandy in occupied France.

The invasion was a success. By late July, Allied troops were marching across France. In August, the French capital of Paris was *liberated* (freed) from the Germans. Within a few months, all of France had been liberated.

The War in Europe Ends

Early in 1945, the Allies invaded Germany. British and American troops attacked Germany from the west. Soviet troops attacked from the east. On April 30, Hitler killed himself. On May 2, Soviet troops captured the German capital of Berlin. And on May 8, Germany's surrender was official. The war in Europe was over.

The Holocaust

When Adolph Hitler came to power in the 1930s, he had ordered the building of **concentration camps** in Europe. Those are large prison camps that can each hold large numbers of prisoners. From the 1930s through World War II, Hitler and his followers ordered millions of Jews and other "enemies" arrested and placed in the camps.

In Poland, Czechoslovakia, Russia, Belgium, France, and elsewhere, German troops rounded up whole neighborhoods of Jews and sent them to the camps.

As the Allies marched through Germany and eastern Europe, they entered the concentration camps. All the fighting and death the soldiers had seen had not prepared them for what they found there.

At some camps, soldiers found bodies stacked like firewood. The bodies were covered with terrible cuts and bruises. The soldiers also found large rooms that had been used as gas chambers. Hundreds of prisoners at a time had been locked in those rooms and killed with poison gas.

The survivors of the camps looked like living skeletons. They told stories of men, women, and children being starved, tortured, and shot.

Twelve million "enemies" of Germany died in the concentration camps. About half of them were Jews.

Today, the murder of six million Jews by the Nazis is known as the **Holocaust**. A holocaust is the complete destruction of something, usually by fire. For Jews, the Holocaust meant destruction of entire families and villages. They were destroyed not by fire, but by prejudice and hate.

Looking Back

1. How did D-Day help lead to Germany's surrender in the war?
2. What was the Holocaust?

This photograph shows General MacArthur and Philippine officers wading to shore after Americans took back the Philippines.

The War in Asia

On April 12, 1945, Franklin Roosevelt died. Vice-President **Harry Truman** took his place. By then, the war in Europe was almost over. But in Asia, victory still seemed far away.

Japan's Advance in the Pacific Is Stopped

After the Japanese attacked Pearl Harbor in 1941, they had moved quickly through the Pacific. Within weeks, they had captured the American island of Guam and Wake Island in the Pacific. By early 1942, they controlled all the major islands in the Pacific, including the Philippine Islands, much of China, and all of Southeast Asia. Nothing seemed to stop the Japanese in their advance through the Pacific. Americans were fearful that the Japanese would attack New Zealand and Australia, then Hawaii and California.

But the United States Navy won two important sea battles that stopped the Japanese advance in the Pacific. Those victories ended the Japanese threat to New Zealand, Australia, Hawaii, and the west coast of the United States. In May 1942, the United States Navy defeated a Japanese fleet in the Coral Sea, northeast of Australia. A month later, another American fleet defeated a Japanese fleet near the Midway Islands.

Island-hopping in the Pacific

Japanese forces were spread across the Pacific on dozens of islands that lay between the United States and Japan. Those islands provided strong defense for Japan.

American military leaders decided on a plan of attack that would weaken the Japanese forces in the Pacific. The plan came to be called *island-hopping*. According to the plan, United States forces would capture only certain key islands. Those islands would then become bases from which to attack other islands. As each island fell, the American forces would move closer to Japan, until they could finally invade it.

In 1943 and 1944, American forces captured key islands of the Solomon, Gilbert, and Marshall Islands. In October 1944, Americans under the command of General **Douglas MacArthur** landed in the Philippines. Later that month, the American navy destroyed a Japanese fleet at Leyte Gulf in the Philippines. That defeat left the Japanese fleet almost powerless in the Pacific. By early 1945, General MacArthur had taken back the Philippines. He then prepared for the invasion of Japan.

By spring 1945, American forces had captured the island of Okinawa, about 350 miles south of Japan. American planes began to bomb Japanese cities regularly.

Looking Back

1. Once the Japanese controlled major islands of the Pacific, where did Amercians fear Japan would attack?
2. How did American forces plan to defeat the Japanese in the Pacific?
3. *Map work*: Look at the map at the top of the next page. What countries and islands were under Japanese control?

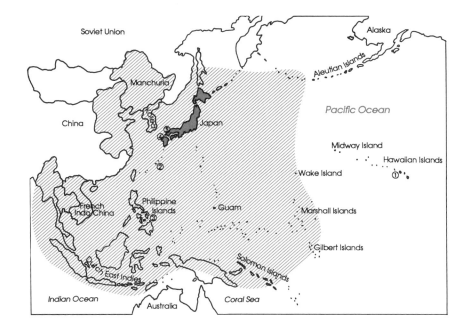

THE WAR IN THE PACIFIC 1942

/////// **Under Japanese control**
① **Pearl Harbor**
② **Okinawa**
③ **Leyte Gulf**
④ **Nagasaki**
⑤ **Hiroshima**

America Decides to Use the Atomic Bomb

The invasion of Japan never took place.

In 1942, President Roosevelt had ordered work to begin on a secret project. The project was called the **Manhattan Project**, and its goal was to build a new kind of weapon that was more destructive than anything known—an **atomic bomb**.

In July 1945, the first atomic bomb was tested in the desert of New Mexico. It was the world's first *nuclear weapon*. The explosion was more powerful than 19,000 tons of TNT. It could be seen miles away.

President Harry Truman decided to use the atomic bomb against Japan if necessary to bring an end to the war. In late July, the Allies warned Japan that it faced total destruction if it did not surrender. But Japanese leaders refused to surrender.

The War Ends in Asia

On August 6, 1945, a single plane dropped an atomic bomb on the city of Hiroshima, Japan. Hiroshima was destroyed in one bright flash. Seventy thousand people died in a matter of seconds.

On August 9, a second atomic bomb was dropped on Nagasaki, Japan. When the explosion was over, more than 40,000 people were dead.

On August 14, Japan surrendered. And on September 2, 1945, Japanese officials signed a treaty of surrender.

The War Took Millions of Lives

World War II was finally over. It had been the most destructive war the world had ever known. Millions had died in the fighting, in the bombings of the cities, and from disease and starvation. Historians believe that more than 55 million military and civilian people all over the world died during the war.

The bombings of Hiroshima and Nagasaki ended the war. But they also brought the world into the nuclear age— an age in which people live with a new kind of fear. People still argue about the use of the atomic bombs in World War II. And they argue about the construction of more nuclear bombs today by governments all over the world.

Looking Back

1. How did the Manhattan Project help end the war and change the world?
2. How did the United States force Japan to surrender?

Chapter 24

Review

Facts First

Use words below to complete each sentence.

atomic bombs	**island-hopping**
concentration camps	**Japan**
D-Day	**Pearl Harbor**
hard times	**territories**
Harry Truman	**World War II**

1. Mussolini and Hitler rose to power during _____ in Europe after World War I.
2. In Asia, military leaders ruled _____.
3. Japan, Italy, and Germany seized _____ belonging to other nations.
4. _____ began in Europe after Germany invaded Poland.
5. The United States entered the war after Japan attacked _____.
6. On _____, Allied forces landed in Normandy and began the liberation of France.
7. Allied troops found _____ where millions of Jews had been murdered.
8. The Allied plan to approach Japan by capturing Pacific islands was called _____.
9. _____ became President when Franklin Roosevelt died.
10. President Truman ordered _____ dropped on Japan.

Word Check

Write the meanings of each of these words. Then use each word in a sentence.

aggression	**ration**
dictator	**totalitarian**

Skill Builder

Find out more about these people and events of the war years.

Irving Berlin	Manzanar
Iva D'Aquino (Tokyo Rose)	Office of Strategic Services (OSS)
Anne Frank	A. Philip Randolph
Executive Order 8802	Raoul Wallenberg
International Red Cross	United Service Organization (USO)

Chapter 24 Notes

Read over the chapter. Find answers to these questions:

1. Who were the dictators of Germany, Italy, and Japan? How did they rise to power?
2. How did World War II begin?
3. Why did the United States join in the fighting in 1942?
4. What was the Holocaust?
5. Why did Japan surrender in 1945?

Be a Historian

Interview someone who remembers World War II. Ask him or her what life was like during the war years.

Bonus

These words and expressions became well known to Americans during World War II. Find out what they mean. Look them up in a dictionary or an encyclopedia. Or ask someone who remembers World War II about them.

blackout curtain	kamikaze
black market	paratrooper
Flying Fortress	radar
GI	V-J Day
jeep	walkie-talkie

Unit 8  **Review**

What Do You Know?

Complete each sentence by choosing the correct ending.

1. In the 1920s, American businesses
   a. were under tight government control.
   b. grew rapidly.
   c. were mostly small companies.

2. Industries in the 1920s improved productivity
   a. through efficiency and the use of electric machines.
   b. when products were made by hand.
   c. by using slaves as workers.

3. Most American workers in the 1920s
   a. made less money than ever before.
   b. could not find jobs.
   c. had more free time than ever before.

4. The American economy in the 1930s
   a. grew slowly but steadily.
   b. suffered from a terrible depression.
   c. grew at a record rate.

5. The New Deal was President Roosevelt's plan
   a. to deal with the Great Depression.
   b. to keep America out of World War II.
   c. to win World War II.

6. The United States entered World War II
   a. before Germany attacked Poland.
   b. when Italy attacked Ethiopia.
   c. after Japan attacked Pearl Harbor.

7. American industrial production during World War II
   a. never matched Germany's production.
   b. made the Great Depression worse.
   c. ended the Great Depression and helped the Allies win the war.

8. World War II ended when the United States
   a. invaded Japan.
   b. dropped atomic bombs on Japan.
   c. surrendered to Germany and Japan.

What Do You Think?

In 1945, President Truman decided to use the atomic bomb against Japan to end the war. Today, some people think Truman should *not* have used the bomb. What do you think? Why?

Skill Builder

Find the years in which these events took place. Write those years beside the events.
- Mussolini comes to power in Italy.
- The stock market crashes.
- Franklin Roosevelt is elected President.
- Hitler comes to power in Germany.
- World War II begins.
- The United States enters World War II.
- World War II ends.

Unit 8 Notes

Look over the unit to find answers to these questions:

1. How did the use of assembly lines affect the automobile industry and other industries?
2. What was the Great Depression and how did it start?
3. What was the New Deal and how did it help Americans?
4. Why did Britain and France declare war on Germany in 1939?
5. What made Japan surrender to the Allies in 1945?

Word Builder

Write a story about World War II. Use as many of these key words as you can.

Key Words

aggression	ration
assemble	totalitarian
dictator	welfare

unit 9   The Nuclear Age

Washington, D.C., and Paris, France 1946

President Truman makes up his mind. He wants Eleanor Roosevelt to become a delegate to a new world organization, the United Nations (UN). Mrs. Roosevelt is the widow of President Franklin Roosevelt.

Other delegates beg President Truman not to appoint a woman. But he calls Mrs. Roosevelt anyway. She agrees to represent her country. Mrs. Roosevelt believes the UN is the one hope for peace in the world.

There are not many women at the UN in 1946. Mrs. Roosevelt shows that women belong in the world organization. In 1946, she is asked to be head of the United Nations Human Rights Commission. Its first job is to write an international bill of rights.

The commission members meet for months in Paris. Progress is slow. Getting people from different nations to agree is not easy. During the meetings, the Soviet delegates criticize the United States.

One day, Dr. A.P. Pavlov of the Soviet Union begins a long speech criticizing the United States. To Mrs. Roosevelt, his words go on and on. They never stop.

Mrs. Roosevelt sees that the delegates are not listening. She watches Pavlov closely. At last, he stops to take a breath. She bangs her gavel.

Mrs. Roosevelt speaks. She tells the delegates they are meeting to work for human rights, not "to attack each other's governments." Pavlov stares at her in surprise. Mrs. Roosevelt bangs the gavel again. "Meeting adjourned!"

Many more meetings follow. In 1948, the Universal Declaration of Human Rights is finally finished. It lists rights that all people in the world should be able to expect.

In Our Time

After World War II, Eleanor Roosevelt dedicated the rest of her life to working for peace. During those years, weapons even more destructive than the atom bomb were invented. And the conflict between the Soviet Union and the United States made people fearful that another world war might break out.

Today, weapons exist that have the power to destroy the world. What are nations doing to make the world a safer, more peaceful place?

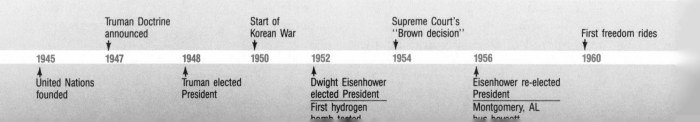

1945	1947	1948	1950	1952	1954	1956	1960
	Truman Doctrine announced		Start of Korean War		Supreme Court's "Brown decision"		First freedom rides
United Nations founded		Truman elected President		Dwight Eisenhower elected President		Eisenhower re-elected President	
				First hydrogen bomb tested		Montgomery, AL bus boycott	

Chapter 25 **American Foreign Policy After the War**

The United Nations headquarters was built in New York City in 1952.

After World War I, Americans did not want to become involved in the problems of other nations. The United States returned to a policy of isolationism.

But after World War II, the United States could not isolate itself from the rest of the world. The war had destroyed cities and towns throughout Europe and Asia. Millions of people around the world were hungry and homeless. Other nations needed America's help to recover from the war.

The democratic nations of the world also faced a new threat after the war—the expansion of the Soviet Union. Democratic nations needed America's help to stop Soviet expansion.

- What was the purpose of the United Nations?
- How did the United States stop Soviet expansion in Europe?
- How did the United States help countries in Asia and the Middle East?

Key Words   You will be using these words in this chapter. Look them up in the glossary at the back of Part 2.

capitalism	**human rights**
communism	**refugee**

The United Nations Is Created

"We seek peace—enduring peace. More than an end to war, we want to end the beginnings of all wars."
President Franklin Roosevelt wrote those words just before his death in 1945. He also wrote that America's survival depends on "the ability of peoples of all kinds to live together and work together in the same world, at peace."

Creating a New World Organization

During World War II, President Roosevelt and other leaders began work on a new world organization. It would replace the League of Nations. Its purpose would be to keep peace and help build a better world after the war. The new organization was called the **United Nations** (**UN**).

In April and May 1945, delegates from 50 nations met in San Francisco, California. Their job was to write a *charter*, or plan, for the UN. They had many disagreements. For example, delegates from small nations argued that large nations had too much power in the UN. But the delegates worked out their differences. On June 26, 1945, the **United Nations Charter** was approved.

The Charter described how the UN would be organized. It also listed the goals of the UN. The most important goal was to end wars and keep peace among nations. A second goal was to protect the rights of all people. A third goal was to improve people's lives around the world.

Looking Back

1. What is the purpose of the UN?
2. What are three goals that the Charter lists for the UN?

How the UN Works

The United Nations Charter set up six main *bodies*, or groups, in the UN. The largest body is the **General Assembly**. It is made up of delegates from each member nation.

The General Assembly meets for several weeks each year to discuss world problems that member nations have.

The General Assembly can give advice. It can also recommend action. But it cannot force nations to go along with its recommendations.

The Security Council Keeps the Peace

The **Security Council** is another United Nations body. Its job is to keep peace in the world. The Council has five *permanent* members: Great Britain, France, China, the Soviet Union, and the United States. The Council also has ten *temporary* members that serve for two years. They are elected by the General Assembly.

Any member nation that has a problem with another nation can come to the Council. The Council tries to settle the problem. It may ask the two nations to meet and work out a solution. Or it may ask the nations to accept a solution that the Council works out. But the Security Council has never forced nations to accept its recommendations.

If war breaks out, the Security Council tries to end the fighting. It may send a **peacekeeping force** into a troubled area. That force is made up of troops from UN nations.

Other UN Bodies

Other UN bodies help to carry out the goals of the UN.

The **Economic and Social Council** works to improve people's lives around the world.

The **International Court of Justice**, or World Court, hears cases that concern international law.

The **Trusteeship Council** helps colonies and territories become independent nations.

And the **Secretariat** is a group of workers, such as secretaries and clerks, who help other UN bodies.

The UN Agencies

The United Nations also has many *agencies*, or organizations. One of them is the **World Health Organization (WHO)**. Its job is to improve the health of people, especially in poor countries. WHO sends doctors, nurses, and health care workers into many countries.

Other agencies help in different ways. The **Food and Agriculture Organization (FAO)** helps the world produce more and better food. The **United Nations Children's Fund (UNICEF)** helps feed and educate children in poor countries.

Protecting Human Rights

In 1948, the General Assembly approved the **Universal Declaration of Human Rights**. The declaration stated that all people have certain *human rights* that should be respected by ''all peoples and all nations.''

The Declaration of Human Rights listed many rights found in the American Bill of Rights. It called for freedom of religion, fair trials, and an end to torture and cruel forms of punishment. It also stated that people have the right to an education and to leisure time.

Nations in the UN agreed to protect the human rights listed in the Declaration of Human Rights.

Looking Back

1. What does the UN General Assembly do?
2. How does the UN Security Council try to keep the peace?
3. What did the Universal Declaration of Human Rights say?
4. What are some human rights described in the Declaration of Human Rights?

Soviet Expansion in Europe

After World War II, a new conflict began: the **cold war**. Countries in the cold war did not actually fight. But they were ready to do so. On one side were the United States and its democratic allies. On the other side were the Soviet Union and other *communist* countries.

Communist countries follow a political system called ***communism***. Communism is based on the idea that all people should share their nation's wealth equally. There should be no *social classes*, or groups of people who are rich or well-off or poor. Everyone should work together for the good of the nation.

Under communism, people do not practice free enterprise or ***capitalism***: A person usually cannot buy or sell property, own a business, or invest in stocks. Almost all property and businesses are owned and run by the government.

Communism in Russia

Russia was the first country to become communistic. In 1917, the Communist Party seized power and set up a government. Russia was renamed the **Union of Soviet Socialist Republics** (**USSR**). It is often called just the *Soviet Union*.

V.I. Lenin, the leader of the Communist Party, became dictator. Under him, the communist government became totalitarian.

In 1924, **Joseph Stalin** became dictator. Stalin used terrorism to increase his control. During Stalin's long rule, millions of Soviet people were arrested and killed. Basic rights such as freedom of speech, freedom of the press, and the right to a fair trial were abolished. Churches were closed and religious leaders arrested.

Lenin and Stalin believed that communism should spread throughout the world. They encouraged people in other countries to revolt and set up communist governments.

Communism Spreads to Eastern Europe

During World War II, the Soviet Union had been greatly damaged by German armies. When the war ended, Stalin wanted to protect the Soviet Union from ever being invaded again. To do that, he had to control the countries near it.

In the last two years of World War II, Soviet troops had fought the Germans in eastern Europe and had taken over the countries there. At the end of the war, the Soviet Union set up communist governments in those countries and made them its *satellites*—nations completely controlled by the Soviet Union.

An Iron Curtain Falls on Eastern Europe

The Soviet Union cut off communications between its satellites and western Europe. People from western Europe could not travel in communist eastern Europe. And eastern Europeans were not allowed to leave the communist countries.

In 1946, Winston Churchill said an "**iron curtain**" had fallen across Europe. That curtain separated Russia and its Soviet satellites from the democratic, or *free*, nations of the world.

Americans Oppose the Soviet Union

Americans were against the Soviet Union. Its political system was not democratic. It did not protect people's individual rights and freedoms.

Americans saw communism as a threat. It threatened free enterprise and capitalism. And it threatened to take over all governments in the world—including America's.

Looking Back

1. What was the cold war?
2. How did communism spread into eastern Europe?
3. Why did Americans oppose the USSR?

American Policy in Europe

President Truman and his advisors believed that the United States should try to keep communism from spreading. So, American foreign policy was developed to *contain* communism—keep it in eastern Europe and out of other European countries.

The Truman Doctrine

In 1947, President Truman spoke before Congress. He said that the United States should ''support free peoples'' in Europe. The United States should provide money, military supplies, and other aid to nations that were fighting against communism. That idea became known as the **Truman Doctrine**.

The Marshall Plan

World War II damaged the economy of many countries in western Europe. Their people were homeless, hungry, and out of work. Their money was almost worthless. To many of those people, communism seemed to be the answer to their problems.

In 1947, Secretary of State **George Marshall** announced a plan to help the countries of western Europe recover from the war. The plan became known as the **Marshall Plan**.

Under the plan, the United States sent over $10 billion to help rebuild the cities and industries of western European countries. When the economy of those countries became stronger, communism became less popular.

The Berlin Airlift

At the end of World War II, Germany was divided among the four major Allies. Britain, France, and the United States each occupied a western part of the country. The Soviet Union occupied the eastern part.

Each Ally also occupied a part of Berlin, the German capital. Berlin was located in the Soviet part of Germany.

In 1948, Britain, France, and the United States decided to combine the western parts of Germany into a new nation. Stalin then ordered a blockade of roads and rail lines into Berlin. He hoped to gain total control of the capital. He also wanted control of western Germany.

President Truman immediately ordered an *airlift* to Berlin. Every day, American planes flew food, coal, and other supplies to the western parts of the city. Nearly a year later, in May 1949, Stalin gave up his attempt to control all of Berlin. He reopened the roads and rail lines into the city.

New Alliances

In 1949, the United States, Canada, and ten western European nations set up the **North Atlantic Treaty Organization** (**NATO**). They agreed to aid any NATO nation that was attacked.

In 1955, the Soviet Union and its satellite nations created their own alliance. It was called the **Warsaw Pact**. Today, Europe remains divided between NATO and Warsaw Pact nations.

Military Forces Are Built Up

Both the United States and the Soviet Union believed that the cold war could *escalate* (grow) into a real war. They began to build up their military power.

The United States began building a ring of American military bases around the Soviet Union and eastern Europe. Those bases were built in countries that were friendly to the United States. The United States built bases in Europe, Asia, Africa, and the Middle East.

Looking Back

1. What was the Truman Doctrine?
2. What was the Marshall Plan?
3. Why did President Truman order an airlift of supplies to Berlin in 1948?
4. What was the purpose of both the NATO alliance and the Warsaw Pact?

American Policy in Asia

From 1945 to 1952, American troops occupied Japan. The occupation forces were led by General Douglas MacArthur. He became the military governor of Japan.

General MacArthur's job was to make sure that Japan would never again be a military threat. He removed Japan's military leaders from power and he abolished the Japanese army, navy, and air force.

Building a Democratic Government in Japan

General MacArthur was also given the job of building a democratic government in Japan. He set up an occupation government that was under tight American control. He filled government positions with Japanese leaders who supported democracy.

General MacArthur helped the Japanese bring about many reforms. For example, workers were allowed to form labor unions. Large landowners were forced to sell land to farmers. And, for the first time, women were given the right to vote.

With American help, the Japanese wrote a new constitution in 1946. The constitution set up a democratic government in Japan. In 1947, Japanese voters elected a new legislature.

Rebuilding Japan's Economy

During the occupation, the United States helped Japan recover from the war. Americans helped Japan rebuild its factories and merchant fleet. Americans also built schools and colleges in Japan.

In 1952, the United States ended its occupation of Japan. Today, the United States and Japan are allies. Japan has become the most prosperous nation in Asia. And the Japanese economy is one of the strongest in the world.

Opposing Communism in China

During World War II, China was ruled by a group called the **Chinese Nationalists**. The Nationalists had set up a republic in China in 1928. **Chiang Kai-shek** was their leader.

In the 1920s, another group had also formed—the **Chinese Communists**. Their leader was **Mao Tse-tung**. The Communists tried to take over the republic, and war broke out between the two groups. When Japan invaded China in the 1930s, the two groups stopped fighting and joined forces. Their fight to control China began again when World War II ended.

The United States did not want a communist government in China. It supported the Nationalists. The United States sent money and weapons to the Nationalists. But, in 1949, the Nationalists were defeated by the Communists.

America Refuses to Deal with Communist China

Chiang Kai-shek and his supporters fled to the island of Taiwan, off China's southern coast. There, they set up a new Nationalist government.

The Communists took control of China. They set up a totalitarian government called the **People's Republic of China**. The United States refused to deal with that government. Instead, it treated Chiang Kai-shek's government in Taiwan as the official Chinese government.

Looking Back

1. How did General MacArthur bring democracy to Japan?
2. Describe Japan's economy today.
3. How did the fight between the Chinese Nationalists and the Chinese Communists end in 1949?

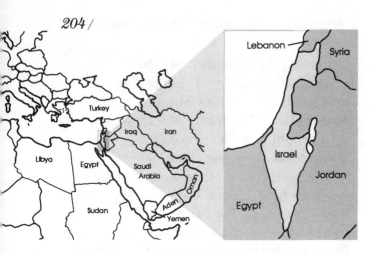

Problems in the Middle East

After World War II, United States foreign policy began to pay more attention to the Middle East. One reason was the discovery that the Middle East was rich in oil. Another reason was the birth of a new nation in the Middle East—Israel.

The UN Sets Up the Nation of Israel

After World War II, thousands of Jewish *refugees* left Europe for Palestine in the Middle East. Many of the refugees had survived the Nazi concentration camps. They were seeking a place where they could be safe from prejudice and persecution.

Those Jews moved to Palestine because they considered it their homeland. Jews had lived in Palestine since biblical times, more than 2000 years before. But Palestine had also been settled by Arab farmers called *Palestinians*. Their culture and religion were very different from the Jews.' The Palestinians also considered Palestine their homeland. They fought to keep the Jewish immigrants out.

Palestine was under British control. But Britain could not keep peace between the Jews and the Palestinians. Britain asked the United Nations to end the dispute. In 1947, the General Assembly voted to divide Palestine: Part of it would become the Jewish nation of Israel. The rest would become a new Arab nation, Palestine.

The First Arab-Israeli War

The Jews accepted the UN plan to divide Palestine. In 1948, the nation of Israel was founded, and the British left Palestine. But the Palestinians would not accept the plan. In 1948, five Arab nations joined the Palestinians in an attack on Israel. The UN Security Council sent a peacekeeping force to stop the fighting, but the war continued.

In 1949, Israeli forces drove the Arabs from Israel. The Arabs agreed to end the war. But they refused to accept Israel's right to exist.

Truman's Middle East Policy

President Truman and most Americans supported Israel. Americans had been horrified by the murder of millions of Jews in World War II. Americans believed Jews should have a safe homeland. The United States sent millions of dollars in aid to Israel.

At the same time, President Truman wanted to win the friendship of Arab nations in the Middle East. The United States' NATO allies depended on the Middle East for oil. President Truman also did not want the Soviet Union to take over the Middle East.

The United States sent aid to many Arab countries. Some American money was used to build *irrigation systems*. The systems supplied water to dry areas, creating new farmland. In return for American aid, some Arab governments agreed to let the United States build military bases in their countries.

Looking Back

1. Why did Jewish refugees move to Palestine after World War II?
2. Why did Arabs attack Israel in 1948?
3. Why did the United States send aid to Arab nations?
4. *Map work*: What are some countries of the Middle East?

Chapter 25

Review

Facts First

Choose the *two* endings that can complete each sentence.

1. The United Nations works to
   a. keep peace among nations.
   b. improve people's lives.
   c. build better weapons.
2. The United Nations can
   a. force nations to accept its decisions.
   b. ask nations to work out their differences.
   c. send troops to troubled areas.
3. The communist government of the Soviet Union
   a. became totalitarian.
   b. became democratic.
   c. violated people's rights.
4. After World War II, the Soviet Union
   a. got along well with the United States.
   b. took control of eastern Europe.
   c. became America's enemy.
5. To stop the spread of communism, America
   a. attacked the Soviet Union.
   b. sent aid to democratic nations.
   c. joined NATO.
6. In Asia, the United States helped the
   a. Japanese recover from the war.
   b. Chinese Nationalists fight communism.
   c. Chinese Communists fight against the Nationalists.
7. In the Middle East, the United States
   a. sent aid to Israel.
   b. sent aid to Arab nations.
   c. refused to help Israel.

Word Check

Write the meanings of these words. Then use them in sentences.

capitalism   **human rights**
communism   **refugee**

Skill Builder

Find each of these Middle Eastern nations on the most recent map of the world. Which two nations share a border with the Soviet Union?

Egypt	Kuwait	Syria
Iran	North Yemen	Turkey
Iraq	Qatar	United Arab
Israel	South Yemen	Emirates
Jordan	Sudan	

Chapter 25 Notes

Read over the chapter. Find answers to these questions:

1. What is the purpose of the United Nations?
2. How did communism spread into eastern Europe?
3. What did the United States do to stop the spread of communism?
4. How did the United States help Japan after World War II?
5. What happened in China after World War II?
6. Why did war break out in the Middle East?

Be a Historian

What's happening in the Middle East today? Read a news article about the United States and a Middle Eastern country. Or listen to a news report on television or the radio.

Then give a news report.

Bonus

1. With your classmates, write a Universal Declaration of Human Rights. Include the rights you think *all* people should have.
2. Find out which countries in the world today have communist governments. Make a map showing them.

Chapter 26 Cold War Tensions at Home and Overseas

The United States tested atomic bombs at Bikini Island in the West Pacific. This photograph shows a 1946 test.

During most of the 1950s, cold war tensions between the United States and the Soviet Union increased.

Both nations built up their armed forces and developed more and more destructive weapons. In Asia, fighting broke out between communist forces and United Nations forces. And within the United States, fear of communism led many Americans to believe that communists were trying to take over the American government.

- Why did the United States and the Soviet Union race to build more powerful weapons?
- Why did the United States send troops to Korea?
- How did fear of communism affect the nation in the 1950s?
- What did President Eisenhower do to ease tensions with the Soviet Union?

Key Words   You will be using these words in this chapter. Look them up in the glossary at the back of Part 2.

arms race	hearing
blacklist	summit conference

The Arms Race

Cold war tensions between the United States and the Soviet Union led to a dangerous *arms race* in the 1950s. You read that the United States built the first atomic bombs during World War II. The Soviet Union began building atomic bombs in 1949.

In the early 1950s, the United States began work on an even more powerful nuclear weapon—the **hydrogen bomb**. The hydrogen bomb was thousands of times more powerful than the first atomic bombs.

The Soviets raced to keep up with the United States. By 1953, both nations had tested hydrogen bombs. In the next years, bigger and more destructive hydrogen bombs were built. By 1956, each nation had aircraft that could carry hydrogen bombs to the other's cities.

Nuclear Missiles

In 1957, a dangerous new weapon was added to the arms race. The Soviets tested the first **inter-continental ballistic missile** (**ICBM**). ICBMs are *missiles*, or rockets, that can fly long distances from one continent to another. ICBMs can be armed with nuclear weapons. By 1958, the United States was also testing ICBMs.

ICBMs could fly much faster than bombers, so they were much harder to destroy. ICBMs could bring nuclear destruction to any city in the Soviet Union or the United States: Now neither the Soviet Union nor the United States could protect its people from the horrors of a nuclear attack.

Looking Back

1. What was the arms race?
2. How did ICBMs make the arms race more dangerous?
3. What is your opinion of the arms race? Why do you say that?

The Korean War Begins

KOREA 1953

Korea is located in northeastern Asia, between China and Japan. Japan took control of Korea in 1910. After World War II, the United States and the Soviet Union occupied Korea.

Korea Is Divided

Korea was divided along the *38th parallel.* (Parallels are the lines that go across the width of maps. They are used to help describe the location of places.) Soviet forces occupied Korea north of the 38th parallel. American forces occupied Korea south of the 38th parallel.

The Soviet Union and the United States could not agree on a way to unite Korea under one government. In 1948, Koreans in the South set up a republic, which became known as South Korea. In the North, the Soviets set up a communist nation, which became known as North Korea. By 1949, Soviet and American forces had left Korea.

North Korea Attacks South Korea

In June 1950, the North Korean government sent troops to attack South Korea. The North Koreans wanted to unite all of Korea under its government.

The government of South Korea asked the UN Security Council for help. The Security Council ordered North Korea to end its invasion. The Council also asked UN nations to send troops to help South Korea.

Sixteen nations sent troops to fight the North Koreans. The United States sent the most troops. The Security Council asked President Truman to name a commander of the UN forces. Truman chose General Douglas MacArthur.

MacArthur Takes Command

Early in the war, North Korea won several victories and overran most of South Korea. UN forces held only a small section of South Korea near the city of Pusan.

In September 1950, UN troops took over Inchon, a city far to the north of Pusan.

The North Korean army was between the UN forces at Inchon and at Pusan. By October, the UN forces had pushed the North Koreans back into North Korea.

China Enters the War

General MacArthur wanted to invade North Korea and destroy the North Korean army. With President Truman's approval, UN forces chased the North Koreans across North Korea toward the Chinese border. By November, American forces had reached the Yalu River. The river was the border between Communist China and North Korea.

In November, Communist China entered the war. Hundreds of thousands of Chinese troops were sent across the Yalu River to help the North Koreans. By December, communist forces had driven the UN forces back across the 38th parallel into South Korea.

Looking Back

1. How did Korea become two separate nations?
2. How did the UN help South Korea after North Korea's attack?

AP/Wide World Photos

U.S. Marines move forward in Korea during an attack.

Ending the Korean War

During the winter and spring of 1951, UN and communist forces fought battles along the 38th parallel. Neither side gained much ground.

General MacArthur believed he could win the war by attacking China. He asked President Truman to let him bomb Chinese cities. He also planned to blockade China's seaports.

The President would not let MacArthur expand the war. "Our goal is not war but peace," Truman said. He wanted to begin peace talks with the Chinese and North Koreans. He also feared that an attack on China would bring the Soviet Union into the war. Then the Korean War could become World War III.

Truman Ends MacArthur's Command

General MacArthur would not accept President Truman's decision. He argued for his plan. He tried to persuade Congress that he was right. But the Constitution makes the President commander in chief of America's armed forces. That means the President's orders must be obeyed.

When MacArthur continued to speak out against the President's decision, the President removed General MacArthur as commander of the UN forces in Korea. The President named General Matthew Ridgeway to take his place.

Peace Comes to Korea

In July 1951, peace talks began in Korea. The talks went on for two years. A cease-fire agreement was finally signed on July 27, 1953. Korea remained divided near the 38th parallel. It is still a divided nation today.

In the Korean War, the United Nations acted to end aggression. Still, millions of people Koreans and Chinese, and Americans and other UN soldiers—lost their lives.

Looking Back

1. Why did President Truman remove General MacArthur from command in Korea?
2. What did the United Nations accomplish in the Korean War?
3. In 1951, many Americans believed that President Truman was wrong to "fire" General MacArthur. What do you think? Why?

Fear of Communism at Home

The spread of communism after World War II frightened Americans. Some people began to believe that communists in the United States were plotting to destroy the American government. Many believed that communists had moved into government jobs and were helping the Soviet Union, China, and other communist countries.

The President Calls for Loyalty Checks

In the late 1940s, some Americans began to demand that the federal government look for communists who might be working in the government. President Truman believed that the nation's government workers were loyal. But, in 1947, Truman set up the **Loyalty Review Board**. Its purpose was to check the loyalty of every worker in the federal government.

Between 1947 and 1951, the government investigated three million government workers. Most of the workers were found to be loyal. But a few hundred workers lost their jobs because they were suspected of disloyalty. Some workers were suspected because they liked Russian music or read books about communism.

Congress Looks into Communist Activity

In 1938, the House of Representatives had set up the **House Un-American Activities Committee (HUAC)**. Its job was to investigate the activities of communists and other groups that might be a threat to the government.

In 1947, HUAC began to look for communists in the motion picture business. Movie actors and writers were asked to appear at HUAC *hearings*.

Several actors and writers refused to answer questions at the hearings. They did not think the government had the right to question people about their beliefs. Most of the actors and writers were loyal Americans. But because they would not cooperate with the committee, they were suspected of disloyalty. Several were **blacklisted**. That meant that no one in the motion picture business would hire them.

Spy Cases Increase Fears

In 1948, HUAC began to investigate a government official named **Alger Hiss**. Hiss had worked in the State Department from 1936 to 1947. The State Department carries out the nation's foreign policy.

A witness testified that Hiss was a communist spy. The witness said Hiss had given American military secrets to the Soviet Union. Hiss denied the charges. But, in 1950, he was jailed for *perjury*, or lying to the committee.

In 1950, two other Americans were arrested for spying. They were **Julius and Ethel Rosenberg**. The Rosenbergs were accused of giving information about the atomic bomb to the Soviet Union during World War II. They were found guilty of spying. In 1953, they were executed.

Americans followed the cases of Alger Hiss and the Rosenbergs in the newspapers. The cases increased Americans' fears of communists within their government.

Looking Back

1. Why did Americans fear communism in the 1950s?
2. What did the Loyalty Review Board do?
3. Why were some movie actors and writers blacklisted?
4. Who was Alger Hiss? Who were the Rosenbergs?

McCarthyism

By 1950, fear of communism was widespread in America. People working in many jobs had to take a *loyalty oath*: They had to swear they were loyal to America and to the Constitution. Some businesses investigated the private lives of their workers to make sure they were loyal.

Some Americans objected to the loyalty oaths and investigations. They said those actions violated people's rights. But many Americans believed that the oaths and investigations were needed to protect the nation from communists.

McCarthy Rises to Power

Senator **Joseph McCarthy** of Wisconsin used people's fear of communism to gain power in the government. In 1950, Senator McCarthy gave a speech in Wheeling, West Virginia. During the speech, McCarthy claimed to have uncovered 205 communists working in the State Department.

During the next few years, McCarthy grew more and more powerful. He charged that there were communists working throughout the government. But he rarely had evidence to back up his charges.

Many people were frightened enough of communism to believe McCarthy even without proof. Support for McCarthy grew. Money poured into his Senate office from people worried about communism.

A Few People Speak Out

A few people spoke out against McCarthy for making wild charges with no evidence. They said McCarthy's charges were costing people jobs and ruining people's reputations. But McCarthy accused people who opposed him of being "soft on communism." (McCarthy meant they were supporters of communism.) So, few people had the courage to stand up to McCarthy.

Senator Margaret Chase Smith spoke out against Joseph McCarthy.

One person who did stand up to McCarthy was Senator **Margaret Chase Smith** of Maine. In a speech before the Senate in 1950, Senator Smith said that McCarthy was wrong to accuse people without proof.

McCarthy Falls from Power

In 1954, Senator McCarthy claimed that there were communists in the United States Army. In April, a Senate committee held hearings to investigate McCarthy's claims. Those hearings, called the **Army-McCarthy hearings**, were shown on television.

For the first time, Americans saw Senator McCarthy at work: They saw McCarthy call people disloyal without proof. (Lawyers for the army showed that there was no evidence to support McCarthy's charges.) They saw him insult patriotic military officers on the witness stand.

The Army-McCarthy hearings led to McCarthy's fall from power. McCarthy lost the support of most Americans. He was criticized by members of the Senate for his conduct. McCarthy's career was ruined.

McCarthy's name has become part of our language: *McCarthyism* means making charges against people without evidence.

Looking Back

1. How did Joseph McCarthy become powerful?
2. How did television turn many Americans against McCarthy?
3. What does *McCarthyism* mean?

Easing Cold War Tensions

The year of 1952 was a presidential election year. President Truman decided not to run for re-election.

The Democratic Party nominated Governor **Adlai Stevenson** of Illinois for President. The Republican Party nominated General Dwight Eisenhower for President.

Eisenhower was very popular with Americans. He had been the commander of Allied forces in Europe during World War II. Americans considered him a war hero. Eisenhower won the election for President by over six million votes.

In 1956, Eisenhower ran for re-election. Again, his opponent was Adlai Stevenson. Eisenhower defeated Stevenson by an even greater margin than before.

Fears of a Nuclear War

In the 1950s, the United States and the Soviet Union were involved in an arms race. The arms race worried many people. They feared it would lead to a nuclear war between those two world powers.

President Eisenhower understood the danger of the arms race and the horrors of nuclear war. He said that in a nuclear war "there can be no truly successful outcome." The President meant that, in a nuclear war, neither side would come out the winner.

The Geneva Summit Conference

In 1955, the President tried to ease tensions between the United States and the Soviet Union. He attended a ***summit conference*** in Geneva, Switzerland. A summit conference is a special meeting of world leaders.

President Eisenhower met with the leaders of the Soviet Union, Britain, and France. They talked about the arms race and other world problems. But they could not agree on what to do about the problems.

Suspending Nuclear Tests

The summit conference of 1955 led to other meetings among Soviet, American, and British leaders. They discussed a ban on the testing of nuclear weapons.

Nuclear weapons were tested far from where people lived. But the tests were still dangerous: Nuclear explosions produced *fallout*, or radioactive dust, which could be blown to areas where people lived.

The United States, the Soviet Union, and Britain could not reach a final agreement to ban the testing. In 1957, they agreed to *suspend* (stop) testing until a final agreement could be reached.

By 1959, tensions between the United States and the Soviet Union had eased. President Eisenhower invited **Nikita Khrushchev**, the Soviet leader, to visit America. During his two-week visit, Khrushchev visited American farms and factories and talked to the nation's leaders.

The Soviets Shoot Down a U.S. Plane

In 1960, relations between the United States and the Soviet Union again became tense. The Soviet Union shot down an American plane that was flying over Soviet territory. The plane, called a *U-2*, carried equipment that could take pictures of Soviet military bases from high in the air.

Khrushchev demanded that President Eisenhower apologize for using U-2 planes to spy on the Soviet Union. The President refused to apologize.

As the 1960s began, the United States and the Soviet Union were once again bitter enemies.

Looking Back
1. Why did the arms race worry people
2. What was the Geneva Summit Conference of 1955?
3. Why did relations between the United States and the Soviet Union become worse in 1960?

Chapter 26

Review

Facts First

Use words below to complete each sentence.

disloyalty	**Joseph McCarthy**
Douglas MacArthur	**Nikita Khrushchev**
Dwight Eisenhower	**nuclear weapons**
HUAC hearings	**South Korea**

1. Both the United States and the Soviet Union built _____ during the arms race.
2. During the Korean War, UN forces helped _____ remain an independent nation.
3. _____ was the commander of UN forces in Korea.
4. Fear of communism led to the _____ in America.
5. Government workers suspected of _____ often lost their jobs.
6. _____ used people's fear of communism to gain power.
7. _____ was elected President in 1952 and 1956.
8. President Eisenhower invited _____, the Soviet leader, to visit the United States.

Word Check

Write the meanings of these words. Then use them in sentences.

arms race	**hearing**
blacklist	**summit conference**

Be a Historian

Find out about relations between the Soviet Union and the United States today. Read newspapers or news magazines. Or listen to the news. Then report what you learned.

Skill Builder

Find out in what years these events happened. Then write them in order.
- The Soviet Union tests the first ICBM.
- The Korean War begins.
- Soviets shoot down an American U-2 plane.
- The Korean War ends.
- The House Un-American Activities Committee investigates the motion picture business.
- President Eisenhower attends the summit conference in Geneva.

Chapter 26 Notes

Read over the chapter. Find answers to these questions:

1. Why was the arms race dangerous?
2. Why did the United States send troops to South Korea?
3. Why did President Truman fire General MacArthur?
4. How did the government fight communism within the United States?
5. What is McCarthyism?
6. How did President Eisenhower try to ease cold war tensions?

Bonus

Many movies have been made about what the world would be like after a nuclear war. Some of those movies are listed below. Watch one of them on televison or video tape. Then discuss it in class.

The Bedford Incident	*On the Beach*
The Day After	*Planet of the Apes*
Dr. Strangelove	*Testament*
Fail Safe	*Threads*

Chapter 27 American Life After the War

Courtesy of The Coca-Cola Company

Coke scores points for pleasure...*anytime*

You add a cheerful lift to family fun when you have ice-cold Coke on hand... So many moments call for Coca-Cola; how good it is to know you have Coca-Cola there. So pleasant in its own distinctive way... Coke is the best-loved sparkling drink in all the world. Enjoy the great taste that is always in the best of taste... Have a Coke!

SIGN OF GOOD TASTE

For many Americans, life after World War II was good: Business was booming. Jobs were plentiful. Americans had money to spend and plenty of goods to buy. Millions of Americans married, began families, and settled down to a quiet life in the suburbs.

But for other Americans, life after the war was difficult. Many Blacks did not share in the nation's prosperity. Blacks were usually given the poorest jobs, housing, and education. By the end of the 1950s, Blacks were demanding their rights and a share of the good life in America.

- Why did the economy remain strong after the war?
- How did metropolitan areas develop in the 1950s?
- How did the civil rights movement begin?
- Why did Americans call for reforms in schools in the late 1950s?

Key Words   You will be using these words in this chapter. Look them up in the glossary at the back of Part 2.

appeal   **discriminate**
consumer   **suburb**

This advertisement was printed in the 1950s.

An Age of Affluence

When World War II ended, Americans feared that the prosperity of the war years would also end. But that did not happen. Instead, the nation began a period of prosperity—an age of *affluence*, or wealth.

The Economy Grows

During the war, the federal government paid billions of dollars to America's businesses. Factories worked night and day making war goods. After the war, people expected government spending to drop sharply. That would mean fewer jobs and a slowdown in the economy.

Instead, government spending almost doubled. Between 1947 and 1957, the federal government spent billions of dollars, much of it on military supplies to fight the cold war. And state and local governments increased their spending too.

Spending by **consumers** also increased after the war. During the war, many people earned good wages, but there were few goods to buy. So, people saved their money.

After the war, factories began making peacetime goods again, such as automobiles and washing machines. Americans eagerly bought those goods. Consumer spending helped the economy grow.

Higher wages also helped increase consumer spending. The growing businesses of the 1950s were paying the highest wages in the nation's history. Labor unions were also strong during the 1950s. Unions won pay raises for many workers.

Looking Back

1. Why did the economy grow after the war?
2. Why did consumer spending increase?

Life in the Age of Affluence

During the depression and the war years, many families were small. After the war, families began getting larger.

Beginning in 1946, the number of babies born each year kept rising. The increase in births was called the **baby boom**. It continued into the 1960s.

The baby boom was good for business. Spending on diapers, baby food, cribs, toys, and children's clothes increased.

Growing Families Need Housing

The baby boom also helped the housing industry grow. The depression had left the nation with a housing shortage. Not many people in the 1930s could afford to build houses. Young married couples often lived with parents.

During World War II, the housing shortage got worse. Making weapons was more important than building houses. And there was a shortage of materials and workers.

As families grew larger after the war, they needed more space. Millions of new homes were built on inexpensive land in the *suburbs*.

Americans Move to the Suburbs

The high wages of the 1950s meant that many families could now afford a home in the suburbs. *Veterans* could also borrow money from the government to buy a house through the **GI Bill**. (Congress passed the GI Bill in 1944. That law gave benefits to Americans in the Armed Forces during the war.)

During the 1950s, millions of Americans moved to the suburbs. Many believed that suburbs were a better place to raise a family than cities. Suburbs were quieter and less crowded. And they were usually safer and cleaner.

This U.S. postage stamp honors World War II veterans.

New Leisure-Time Activities

During the 1950s, many families had time and money to enjoy new leisure-time activities. By 1950, many workers had a 40-hour work week. They had two-day weekends and two weeks of paid vacation a year.

Many people enjoyed new sports such as waterskiing in their leisure time. Sales of camping equipment and sporting goods rose. Book sales also increased. Americans had begun buying inexpensive paperback books during the war. After the war, more and more paperback books became available.

Teenagers spent time listening to a new kind of music—*rock 'n' roll*. Rock 'n' roll performers, such as **Elvis Presley** and **Buddy Holly**, were very popular.

Television Enters the Home

The nation's favorite new leisure-time activity was watching television. Most people had never seen television in 1945. But by 1960, Americans had bought over 60 million television sets. By then, the average person spent six hours a day watching television.

Television entertained viewers with everything from dramatic plays to professional wrestling. People could also watch the news and see their political leaders on television.

Television helped the economy too. Television commercials persuaded Americans to spend money on everything from soap to cough drops.

Looking Back

1. What was the baby boom?
2. Why could many Americans afford new homes in the 1950s?
3. Why did many young families move to the suburbs?
4. How did Americans of the 1950s spend their free time?

Left: New neighborhoods such as Levittown, New York, sprang up quickly after World War II ended. *Right*: This photograph shows one of the houses in Levittown.

The Changing American City

In Chapter 10, you read that large numbers of Americans began to move from farms to cities in the early 1800s. The mills and factories of the cities provided people with jobs.

Throughout the 1800s and early 1900s, Americans continued to leave the farms for the cities. But in the 1930s, during the depression, there were few jobs to be found in the nation's cities. So, fewer people left the farms.

During the 1950s, the factories and businesses of the cities were booming again. People began to leave farms and small towns in greater numbers than ever.

By 1960, seven of every ten Americans lived in a *metropolitan area*. A metropolitan area is made up of a large city and the suburbs that surround it.

Whites Move to the Suburbs

Most of the growth in metropolitan areas came in the suburbs. Many of the nation's big cities grew very little during the 1950s. Some, such as Detroit and New York City, lost population.

The people moving out of cities were mostly Whites. New groups moved into the neighborhoods they left behind.

Many of the new city people were southern Blacks. They had moved north looking for work in factories. Two million Blacks left the South from 1940 to 1960.

Other newcomers were immigrants from Mexico and Puerto Rico. By 1960, more Puerto Ricans were living in New York City than in Puerto Rico's capital, San Juan. More Mexicans were living in Los Angeles than in any city in Mexico except its capital.

Many Businesses Leave the Cities

Many city businesses moved to the suburbs during the 1950s. When businesses left, they stopped paying city taxes. Those cities then found it difficult to pay for police and fire protection. They had less tax money to take care of parks, streets, and schools.

When cities lost businesses, they also lost jobs. Newcomers had trouble finding work. Many people living in the nation's cities never enjoyed the prosperity of the 1950s.

Looking Back

1. Why did many Americans move to metropolitan areas during the 1950s?
2. How did big cities change during the 1950s?
3. How were cities hurt when businesses moved to the suburbs?

Blacks Fight Segregation

Rosa Parks arrives at a Montgomery, Alabama, courthouse for her trial. She was fined $14 for failing to move to the segregated section of a bus.

Wherever Blacks lived in the 1950s, they faced prejudice and *segregation*.

In the South, segregation was backed by state laws. Those laws said Blacks could not go to "White" schools. Blacks could not eat in "White" restaurants, sit in the "White" sections of buses, or drink from "White" drinking fountains.

Outside the South, segregation was not usually written into law. But many Whites *discriminated* against Blacks: Landlords in "White" neighborhoods would often not rent to Blacks. Blacks could find housing only in crowded "Black" neighborhoods.

Many White business owners would not hire Blacks. Many labor unions would not let Blacks into their training programs. Blacks could only get low-skilled, low-paying jobs.

Some Blacks tried to get around segregation by starting businesses of their own. They soon found that White bankers would not lend them money to get started. And White landlords would not rent them business space.

Most Blacks Live in Poverty

During the 1950s, Black families earned about half the income of White families.

Martin Luther King, Jr., was a young minister from Atlanta, Georgia. He saw how segregation hurt Blacks. King said Blacks lived "on an island of poverty in the midst of a vast ocean of...prosperity."

A Black Family Fights School Segregation

In 1951, a Black family in Topeka, Kansas, decided to fight segregation in the city's schools. Their daughter was turned away from a school because of her race. With the help of the NAACP, the family sued the Topeka Board of Education. The family's name was *Brown*.

The Browns took their case first to the U.S. District Court. They asked the court to end school segregation. The district court ruled against the Browns. The Browns **appealed** to the U.S. Court of Appeals, then to the U.S. Supreme Court.

In 1954, the Supreme Court decided the case of **Brown v. the Board of Education of Topeka**. The Court ruled that school segregation was unconstitutional. It said the 14th Amendment promises every citizen "equal protection" of the laws. That means laws must treat all people equally. To segregate school children because of their race is not equal treatment.

Federal Troops Enforce Desegregation

In 1955, the Supreme Court ordered segregated schools to *desegregate*, or end segregation, as quickly as possible. At first, many Whites did everything they could to stop desegregation. Black students who tried to enter desegregated schools were often attacked by Whites.

In Little Rock, Arkansas, crowds of angry Whites tried to keep Blacks out of Central High School. President Eisenhower sent troops to Little Rock in 1957. Under the troops' protection, the Black students entered the school.

Desegregation moved slowly during the 1950s. But more of the nation's schools began to open their doors to students of all races.

Looking Back
1. How did state laws support segregation in the South?
2. How did Whites discriminate against Blacks in the North?
3. What did the Supreme Court say about school segregation?

The Civil Rights Movement

During the 1950s, Blacks demanded an end to segregation and discrimination. They called on the government to protect their civil rights. Their fight for equal rights was known as the **civil rights movement**.

Montgomery Blacks Boycott the Buses

Blacks won an important victory against segregation in Montgomery, Alabama. In December 1955, **Rosa Parks**, a Black woman, got on a bus in Montgomery. She took a seat in the ''White'' section of the bus. When the driver ordered Rosa Parks to give her seat to a White passenger, she refused. She was arrested and taken to jail.

Blacks in Montgomery then began a bus boycott. During the next year, 17,000 Blacks refused to ride city buses. They walked or shared car rides.

Blacks also challenged Montgomery's segregated bus system in court. In 1956, the Supreme Court ruled that segregation on buses was unconstitutional. By December 1956, Blacks were sitting wherever they pleased on Montgomery's desegregated buses.

King Becomes a Leader

The bus boycott in Montgomery was led by Martin Luther King. The success of the boycott made him the most important leader in the civil rights movement.

King's life was threatened and his home was bombed. Still, King urged Blacks not to use violence themselves. Instead, he urged Blacks to use *nonviolent protest*, or peaceful protest, to end segregation.

Sit-ins

The success of the Montgomery bus boycott encouraged Blacks to use nonviolent protest against other forms of segregation.

In 1960, Black college students walked into a department store in Greensboro, North Carolina. They sat down at the lunch counter for Whites. When asked to leave, they refused. Instead, they opened their books and began to study. They said they would sit at the counter until they were served. Their protest became known as a **sit-in**.

The students' sit-in proved successful. The lunch counter began to serve Blacks. Soon, Blacks in other cities were using sit-ins to protest segregation at lunch counters and other public places. Thousands of people, most of them Black, were arrested. But the protests continued.

Freedom Rides

Soon, civil rights workers of different races joined together for **freedom rides** across the South. Waiting rooms, restaurants, and restrooms in bus stations were segregated. The freedom riders rode buses from town to town, protesting such segregation.

The freedom riders were often met with violence. They were attacked by angry mobs. They were beaten and arrested. Their buses were burned. But freedom rides continued.

In time, civil rights protests began to change life in the South. ''WHITE'' and ''COLORED'' signs were pulled down from bus station waiting rooms. Restaurants, hotels, and stores no longer refused to serve Blacks.

Looking Back

1. What was the goal of the civil rights movement?
2. How did Blacks use nonviolent protest to fight segregation?

America Enters the Space Age

On October 4, 1957, Americans heard some shocking news: The Soviet Union announced that it had sent a small satellite, called *Sputnik I*, into space. *Sputnik I* was the first man-made object to circle the earth.

A few months later, the Soviets launched *Sputnik II*. It carried a live dog into space.

The launchings of *Sputnik I* and *Sputnik II* surprised Americans. They had always believed that American technology was ahead of Soviet technology. But now the Soviets seemed to be ahead in the building of rockets and satellites.

''Why has the United States fallen behind?'' many Americans asked.

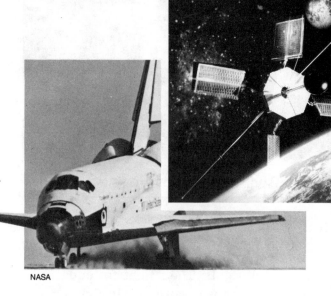

NASA

Top: This satellite was launched in 1967. *Bottom:* This photograph taken in 1985 shows a space shuttle landing.

Americans Call for Reforms in Schools

Some Americans argued that the Soviet Union had taken the lead in technology because Soviet schools were better than American schools. Those Americans argued that Soviet schools were producing better scientists and engineers.

Those who complained about America's schools said that students were spending too much time studying subjects such as music, art, and home economics. Instead, students should be spending more time studying math and science. Many Americans called for reforms in education.

In 1958, Congress passed the **National Defense Education Act**. The Act provided money to public schools to build science labs, buy textbooks, and improve the teaching of math, science, and foreign languages. The Act also provided loans to college students so they could complete their studies.

America Races to Catch Up

Sputnik I and *Sputnik II* gave the Soviet Union an early lead in the *space race*. To the Soviet Union and the United States, success in space meant leadership in science, engineering, and national defense. So, the two countries competed with each other to develop space programs. Each wanted to be the leader in space.

In January 1958, the United States launched its first satellite, *Explorer I*. Two months later, the United States launched another satellite, *Vanguard I*.

In 1958, Congress set up the **National Aeronautics and Space Administration (NASA)**. Its purpose was to develop America's space program. The hard work of NASA scientists and engineers would bring American successes in space in the 1960s and 1970s.

Looking Back
1. Why did the launching of *Sputnik I* surprise Americans?
2. Why did some Americans call for reforms in America's schools?
3. What is NASA?

This U.S. postage stamp honors the U.S. space program.

A DECADE OF ACHIEVEMENT

Chapter 27

Review

Facts First

Use words below to complete each sentence.

baby boom	**protest**
Blacks	**reforms**
businesses	**satellite**
Martin Luther King	**suburbs**
prosperity	**unconstitutional**

1. The 1950s were a time of _____ for most Americans.
2. The increase in the number of babies born in America was called the _____.
3. Many White families moved from the cities to the _____.
4. Cities lost money and jobs when people and _____ moved away.
5. _____ throughout the country faced segregation and discrimination.
6. The Supreme Court ruled that segregation in schools was _____.
7. _____ led a boycott in Montgomery, Alabama, to end segregation on buses.
8. Blacks also used sit-ins and freedom rides to _____ against segregation.
9. The Soviets launched the first _____ in 1957.
10. Many Americans called for _____ in the nation's schools to improve education.

Word Check

Write the meaning of each of these words. Then use each word in a sentence.

appeal	**discriminate**
consumer	**suburb**

Skill Builder

Find out about one of these famous Americans. Then report what you learned.

Agnes De Mille	Walter Reuther
Edna Ferber	Jackie Robinson
Martin Luther King	Bishop Fulton Sheen
Thurgood Marshall	Margaret Chase Smith
Margaret Mead	Adlai Stevenson
Edward R. Murrow	Earl Warren

Chapter 27 Notes

Read over the chapter. Find answers to these questions:

1. Why were the 1950s called an ''Age of Affluence''?
2. Why did many young families move to suburbs?
3. Why did many cities become poorer?
4. How did segregation harm Blacks?
5. How did Blacks fight segregation?
6. Why did some Americans call for changes in education?

Be a Historian

What do Americans protest against today? How do Americans protest?

Cut out a picture from a newspaper or magazine that shows Americans protesting. Paste the picture onto a sheet of paper. On the paper, tell when and where the picture was taken. Also tell what the people in the picture are protesting against.

Bonus

1. Find out how young people looked and dressed in the 1950s. Visit your school library and look through two or three yearbooks from the 1950s. With your class, discuss how styles have changed.
2. Find an early rock 'n' roll record by one of these people: Elvis Presley, Chuck Berry, Buddy Holly, or Bill Haley. (You may borrow it from a public library.) Bring the record to class for your classmates to hear.

Unit 9

CHAIRMAN

Review

What Do You Know?

Choose the *two* endings that can complete each sentence.

1. After World War II, the United States
   a. returned to isolationism.
   b. helped to rebuild Japan.
   c. joined the United Nations.
2. The purpose of the United Nations is to
   a. keep peace in the world.
   b. end communism.
   c. help people everywhere lead better lives.
3. Americans opposed the Soviet government because it
   a. was not democratic.
   b. violated people's rights.
   c. supported Germany in World War II.
4. To contain communism, the United States
   a. sent troops to Korea.
   b. formed an alliance with the Soviet Union.
   c. built military bases in Europe and Asia.
5. The arms race
   a. escalated after World War II.
   b. led to more destructive nuclear weapons.
   c. ended in the 1950s.
6. Many Americans in the 1950s
   a. moved to the suburbs.
   b. earned good wages.
   c. supported communism.
7. Many Black Americans in the 1950s
   a. began to protest against segregation.
   b. moved to the South.
   c. suffered from discrimination.

What Do You Think?

Some people say that nuclear weapons have made the world a safer place. They say that there has been no world war since the 1940s because nations know that it would be a nuclear war. What do you think?

Skill Builder

Find out about one of these countries in an encyclopedia. Show your class where the country is on a map and tell them about the government and people of the country.

COMMUNIST COUNTRIES	FREE COUNTRIES
Czechoslovakia	Denmark
East Germany	Greece
Hungary	Netherlands
People's Republic of China	Turkey
Poland	West Germany

Unit 9 Notes

Look over the unit to find answers to these questions:

1. What is the purpose of the United Nations?
2. What caused a war in the Middle East in 1948?
3. What is communism? Why have Americans feared communist governments?
4. What is the arms race? What is the space race?
5. How did Americans' fear of communism lead to the rise of Senator Joseph McCarthy?
6. How did supporters of the civil rights movement fight segregation in the 1950s and 1960s?

Word Builder

Write a story about a refugee who came to the United States from a communist country in the 1950s. Use as many of these key words as you can.

Key Words

arms race	human rights
communism	refugee
discriminate	summit conference

unit 10 Challenge and Change

Washington, D.C.—August 28, 1963

Martin Luther King stands in front of the Lincoln Memorial. Facing him are thousands of people—Blacks and Whites, rich and poor, young and old. They have come to Washington on a march for civil rights. The Reverend King is a leader of the march.

He begins a speech he has prepared. He speaks about the Emancipation Proclamation, signed by Abraham Lincoln over 100 years ago. He says it was "a great beacon light of hope to millions of Negro slaves.... But one hundred years later, the Negro is still not free."

King says that the Declaration of Independence and the Constitution promise equal rights to all. "*Now* is the time to make real the promises of democracy," he says. "*Now* is the time to make justice a reality for *all* God's children."

The crowd cheers. King puts aside his speech and speaks from his heart: "I say to you today, my friends, that even though we face the difficulties of today and tomorrow, I still have a dream."

"I have a dream," he says, "[that Blacks and Whites] will be able to sit down together at the table of brotherhood."

"I have a dream," he says, "[that people] will not be judged by the color of their skin, but by the content of their character."

"Let freedom ring!" King cries out. "[Let the time come] when all of God's children... will be able to join hands and sing in the words of the old Negro spiritual, 'Free at last! Free at last! Thank God Almighty, we are free at last!'"

In Our Time

The Reverend King challenged Americans to change. He called on Americans to change their ideas about race. But changing old ideas is never easy. Prejudice and discrimination are still problems in America today.

Americans of the future will face many challenges. They may be called upon to change their ideas or their ways of life. How do you think America will change in the years ahead?

John Kennedy elected President		Johnson elected President		Richard Nixon elected President		Gerald Ford becomes President		Ronald Reagan elected President	
1960	1963	1964	1965	1968	1973	1974	1976	1980	1987
	Kennedy assassinated Lyndon Johnson becomes President		American troops in Vietnam		American troops out of Vietnam		Jimmy Carter elected President		Iran-Contra hearings

Chapter 28 **The Troubled Sixties**

President John Kennedy is standing in front of the presidential seal at a news conference in 1963.

UPI/Bettmann Newsphotos

The year of 1960 was an election year. President Eisenhower's term of office was ending, and it was time to elect a new President. The Republican Party nominated Vice-President Richard Nixon as its candidate for President. The Democratic Party chose Senator John Kennedy of Massachusetts.

Kennedy was young and energetic. He was an excellent speaker and campaigner. He defeated Nixon in one of the closest elections in history.

When President Kennedy took office in 1961, the space age had begun. The civil rights movement was growing. The American economy was prosperous. And the United States was one of the "super-powers" of the world. No one could guess that the 1960s would become a decade of trouble and pain for the nation.

• What new frontiers did President Kennedy open for Americans?
• What was President Johnson's Great Society program?
• How did the Black power movement develop in the 1960s?
• Why did many Americans oppose the war in Vietnam?

Key Words You will be using these words in this chapter. Look them up in the glossary at the back of Part 2.

astronaut	**ghetto**
demonstration	**integration**

President Kennedy's New Frontier

During his campaign, **John Kennedy** told Americans that the nation, under his leadership, would conquer *new frontiers*. Problems such as poverty and discrimination had yet to be overcome. And challenges such as improving education and exploring space faced the nation. Those were the new frontiers that Kennedy spoke about.

Kennedy Sets a Goal in Space

In 1961, President Kennedy set a new goal for America's space program—to land an American on the moon before 1970.

Both Russia and the United States had made great progress in the technology of space travel. The first man in space, Russian cosmonaut **Yuri Gargarin,** made a single *orbit*, or circle, around the Earth in April 1961. And, in May, *astronaut* **Alan Shepard** became the first American to be sent into space.

In 1962, **John Glenn** became the first American to orbit the Earth. His spacecraft circled the Earth three times and then landed safely.

The Peace Corps Helps Poor Nations

Another of President Kennedy's programs was the **Peace Corps**. It was a program that sent Americans to poor countries to help people there.

Thousands of teachers, nurses, farmers, engineers, and others joined the Peace Corps. They went to countries in Asia, Africa, and Latin America. They helped people learn to do such things as build dams, grow more food, and improve health care.

Today, the Peace Corps is still working to help other countries.

Looking Back
1. What were President Kennedy's new frontiers?
2. What was the Peace Corps?

The Kennedy Years

When President Kennedy took office in 1961, relations between the United States and the Soviet Union had grown tense. Each country was convinced that the other was ready to attack. So, each continued to secretly develop more powerful military equipment and nuclear weapons.

The Cuban Missile Crisis

In 1959, the government of Cuba had been overthrown in a revolution led by **Fidel Castro**. Castro had then set up a communist government that was friendly with the Soviet Union. The United States opposed Castro's government. Americans feared that communism would spread from Cuba into Central and South America.

In October 1962, President Kennedy learned that the Soviet Union was building missile bases in Cuba. He announced that the United States would not allow Soviet missile bases so close to the United States. He ordered the navy to blockade Cuba and to turn back Soviet ships. The President also demanded that the missile bases in Cuba be torn down.

For six days, people all over the world waited tensely as Soviet ships moved toward Cuba. People feared that the crisis between the two superpowers of the world would end in a nuclear war. Then, on October 28, Soviet leader Nikita Krushchev ordered the Soviet ships to turn back. He also ordered the missile bases in Cuba to be torn down.

Tensions Ease

Both President Kennedy and Premier Krushchev were alarmed at how close their nations had come to war. When the missile crisis was finally over, the two leaders took steps to improve relations between their countries.

This coin was issued to honor the first 200 years of the United States. John Kennedy is pictured on one side; Independence Hall is on the other.

A telephone line was set up between Washington, D.C., and Moscow. The set-up was called the "hot line." In any future crisis, American and Soviet leaders could talk to each other quickly and directly.

The United States, the Soviet Union, and Great Britain also began new talks aimed at banning nuclear weapons tests. In July 1963, the three nations signed a treaty banning nuclear tests in the atmosphere. The treaty, however, allowed underground tests to continue.

President Kennedy Is Assassinated

On November 22, 1963, President Kennedy and Mrs. Kennedy were in Dallas, Texas, with Vice-President **Lyndon Johnson** and Mrs. Johnson. The President and the Vice-President were in Texas to win support for their re-election in 1964.

While riding through the city in an open car, President Kennedy was shot and killed.

Lyndon Johnson Becomes President

Through the shock and confusion of the time, the nation's government continued to work: Within hours of President Kennedy's death, the nation had a new leader. Vice-President Lyndon Johnson was sworn in as President.

Looking Back

1. What was the Cuban missile crisis?
2. What did the United States and the Soviet Union do to ease tensions after the missile crisis?
3. Has there been an international crisis in recent times that was like the Cuban missile crisis? Why do you say that?

President Johnson's Great Society

When President Johnson took office, he promised to carry out President Kennedy's goals. Congress had not gone along with President Kennedy on many of his programs. But President Johnson knew how to work with members of Congress to get bills passed—he had spent 25 years as a member of Congress.

Congress Passes a Civil Rights Bill

In 1963, President Kennedy had asked Congress to pass a bill to end segregation and discrimination. Thousands of Americans, led by Martin Luther King, had marched to Washington in support of the bill. But Congress did not pass it. In 1964, President Johnson convinced Congress to approve the bill. It was called the **Civil Rights Act of 1964**.

The Civil Rights Act of 1964 protected the voting rights of all Americans, including Blacks and others who had been kept from voting. It also outlawed segregation in public places, such as parks, restaurants, hotels, theaters, and hospitals. And it outlawed job discrimination: Employers could no longer refuse to hire people because of their race, religion, sex, or because they came from another country.

Johnson Declares War on Poverty

While carrying on President Kennedy's work, President Johnson also created his own programs. In 1964, he called for a "war on poverty" to help the 35 million Americans who were poor.

Congress approved several programs to help poor people. One was the **Head Start** program. It set up nursery schools for children in low-income neighborhoods. Those schools taught the children learning skills that could help them succeed in elementary school.

Another program was the **Job Corps**. It provided summer jobs for high school students from low-income families. It also provided job training for students who had dropped out of school. A third program was called **Volunteers in Service to America (VISTA)**. It was something like the Peace Corps. VISTA workers went to poor communities throughout the United States to help people improve conditions there.

Building a Great Society

In 1964, the next election year, the Democratic Party chose Johnson as its candidate for President. He was elected by a huge majority. President Johnson challenged Americans to build a "great society." He said a great society was a place where all Americans could live "the good life." Johnson's plan to improve life in America became known as the **Great Society** program.

In 1965, the President sent over 60 bills to Congress to help Americans. Congress passed most of those bills into law. Laws were passed to help schools in poor areas. A program was set up to help poor students pay for college. The **Medicare Act** was passed to help older people pay medical bills. And the **Medicaid** program was set up to help poor people of all ages get medical care.

Congress also added a new department to the executive branch of government. It was called the **Department of Housing and Urban Development (HUD)**. HUD helped cities plan and pay for housing projects and other programs for low-income families.

Congress also passed the **Voting Rights Act of 1965**. It gave more protection to people's right to vote.

Looking Back

1. What was the Civil Rights Act of 1964?
2. How did President Johnson's programs carry out a "war on poverty"?
3. How did Congress help the President build a "great society"?

The Fight for Civil Rights Continues

In Chapter 27, you read about the civil rights movement that began in the 1950s. Led by Martin Luther King, it helped bring racial *integration* to the South.

By the early 1960s, the civil rights movement had spread to the rest of the country. Courts throughout the nation struck down segregation laws. State legislatures and Congress passed new laws outlawing discrimination. But for many Blacks, especially those living in Black *ghettos*, those actions did not change their day-to-day lives.

Black Ghettos Explode

In most cities, Blacks could not move into certain neighborhoods because of discrimination. Poor Blacks could only find places to live in Black ghettos—large city neighborhoods of Black people.

The ghettos received few city services. Streets were littered and in need of repairs. Buildings were in bad condition and overrun with rats. People often lived in apartments that were unhealthy and unsafe.

Unemployment was high in the ghettos. Crime was also high. Many Blacks who lived there felt hopeless, trapped, and angry. **Malcolm X**, a Black leader, warned the nation that Black ghettos were "a powder keg" waiting to explode.

In 1965, rioting broke out in Watts, a ghetto in Los Angeles. During the next three years, riots broke out in almost every large city in the United States.

Martin Luther King Is Assassinated

On April 4, 1968, Martin Luther King was assassinated in Memphis, Tennessee. He was shot by a White man. Angry Blacks rioted. Federal troops were called out in Chicago, Baltimore, and other cities.

Blacks Call for Black Power

During the years of the ghetto riots, a new movement gained strength among Blacks. It became known as the **Black power movement**.

Black power leaders said that Blacks should control Black communities. They urged Blacks to use their economic and political power to change their lives. They said Blacks should support Black businesses and build up Black neighborhoods. They also urged Blacks to elect Blacks to office.

The Black power movement encouraged Blacks to take pride in their race and in their history. "Black is beautiful" became a popular saying. Many Blacks showed their racial pride by wearing African dress and taking African names. They also demanded that schools and colleges offer classes on Black history and culture.

Blacks Make Political Gains

Efforts by Blacks to gain political power began to succeed. In 1966, there were only 148 Blacks in state legislatures. Only six Blacks served in Congress. No city had a Black mayor.

By 1973, over 200 Blacks had been elected to state legislatures, and 16 Blacks had been elected to Congress. Black mayors had been elected in cities including Cleveland, Ohio; Los Angeles, California; and Newark, New Jersey.

Looking Back

1. Why did Blacks living in ghettos feel hopeless and angry?
2. What did Black power leaders urge Blacks to do?

The Vietnam War Begins

During the 1960s, the United States again went to war, this time in Vietnam, in Southeast Asia. Vietnam had been a French colony. After World War II, the Vietnamese won their independence. But like Korea, Vietnam was a divided country.

North Vietnam was controlled by a communist government led by **Ho Chi Minh**. South Vietnam became a republic, with **Ngo Dinh Diem** as its president. The United States supported Diem's government.

In 1957, communist guerrillas in South Vietnam began attacks against Diem's government. The communist guerrillas, called the **Vietcong**, wanted to overthrow Diem and unite all of Vietnam under one communist government.

Aid Is Sent to South Vietnam

The communist uprising in South Vietnam alarmed President Eisenhower and other leaders of free nations. If South Vietnam fell to the communists, other nations in Southeast Asia, such as Laos and Cambodia, would also fall.

President Eisenhower used his powers as commander in chief of the armed forces to send several hundred American military advisors to South Vietnam. Their job was to train South Vietnam's army. The United States also sent money, weapons, and other supplies to South Vietnam.

When Kennedy became President, he continued President Eisenhower's policy. President Kennedy sent more advisors and aid to South Vietnam.

By the time President Johnson came into office, in 1963, 16,000 American advisors were in South Vietnam. President Johnson also supported the government of South Vietnam. He believed that American *combat* (fighting) troops were needed in Vietnam to defeat the communist forces.

VIETNAM 1964

U.S. Combat Troops Are Sent to Vietnam

In August 1964, North Vietnamese torpedo boats attacked two American navy ships in the Gulf of Tonkin off North Vietnam's coast. President Johnson said that North Vietnam had attacked United States forces without cause. He said U.S. forces had to be able to defend themselves.

The President sent a bill to Congress called the **Tonkin Gulf Resolution**. Congress approved the bill. The Tonkin Gulf Resolution gave the President the power to "take all necessary measures" to defend American forces in Vietnam. It was not a declaration of war. But the President now had the support of Congress to send combat troops to Vietnam.

In February 1965, President Johnson ordered the air force to bomb North Vietnam. In April, the President sent marines to Vietnam to support the South Vietnamese. By the end of the year, the President had sent nearly 200,000 American fighting troops to Vietnam.

Looking Back

1. Why did war begin in Vietnam?
2. What was the Tonkin Gulf Resolution?
3. How did President Johnson use the Tonkin Gulf Resolution?

The Vietnam War Divides Americans

In the early years of the Vietnam War, most Americans believed that the war was necessary to stop the spread of communism. They also expected the United States to win quickly, since Vietnam was a small country.

But by 1967, ten years after it began, the war was still going on. Many Americans began to speak out against it.

Americans Turn Against the War

Americans who opposed the war were called "doves." Doves believed that billions of American dollars and thousands of American lives were being wasted on a war that the nation could not seem to win.

Doves also said that the United States had no right to be in Vietnam. They said that the war was a *civil* war; therefore, it should be settled by Vietnamese, not by Americans.

The Anti-War Movement Grows

On January 30, 1968, the Vietcong began attacking cities throughout all of South Vietnam. They took part of Saigon, the capital of South Vietnam. The attacks came during *Tet*, the Vietnamese new year, so they were called the *Tet offensive*.

The Tet offensive convinced many Americans that the United States could not win the war—not unless it completely destroyed Vietnam. Throughout 1968, protesters held **demonstrations** across the nation. They demanded that the United States *withdraw* from (get out of) Vietnam. Some of the demonstrations ended in violence. Protesters, supporters of the war, and police troops battled with each other.

President Johnson Decides Not to Run

Many Americans blamed President Johnson for the conflicts in the United States over the war. In March 1968, the President announced that he would not run for re-election.

Vice-President **Hubert Humphrey** and Senator **Robert Kennedy** campaigned to become the Democratic Party's candidate for President. Vice-President Humphrey supported President Johnson's policies in Vietnam. Senator Kennedy did not.

Senator Kennedy was the favorite candidate of many Democrats. He was John Kennedy's brother. He opposed the war. And he supported the civil rights movement.

In June 1968, Senator Kennedy was assassinated while campaigning in California. Once again, Americans were shocked by the tragic loss of a leader.

Violence at the Democratic Convention

In August, the Democratic Party held its national convention in Chicago to nominate candidates for President and Vice-President. Thousands of protesters also went to Chicago to protest against the war.

Chicago police surrounded the anti-war protesters. Millions of Americans watched on television as the demonstrations turned into battles between the police and the protesters.

Nixon Becomes President

The Democrats nominated Hubert Humphrey for President. The Republican Party nominated Richard Nixon.

During his campaign, Nixon said he had a "secret plan" for ending the Vietnam War. He promised to "restore order and respect for the law in America." His campaign slogan "Bring us together" was his promise to end the conflicts that divided the country. Americans were tired of the war, riots, and protests. They elected Richard Nixon President.

Looking Back

1. Why did "doves" oppose the Vietnam War?
2. What were Richard Nixon's campaign promises in 1968?

Chapter 28

Review

Facts First

Use words below to complete each sentence.

Black power	**Lyndon Johnson**
blockade	**Martin Luther King**
communist	**Peace Corps**
Head Start	**Richard Nixon**
John Kennedy	**segregation**

1. In 1960, _____ challenged Americans to conquer "new frontiers," such as space.
2. When the Soviet Union began building missile bases in Cuba, President Kennedy ordered a _____ of Cuba.
3. President Kennedy set up the _____, a program that helped people in poor countries.
4. _____ became President after President Kennedy was assassinated.
5. The Civil Rights Act of 1964 outlawed acts of discrimination and _____.
6. Medicaid and _____ were two of President Johnson's programs to help low-income families.
7. The leader of the civil rights movement was _____.
8. The _____ movement encouraged Blacks to take pride in their race and their history.
9. America opposed the _____ government of North Vietnam.
10. In 1968, _____ became President after saying he had a plan to end the war.

Word Check

Write the meaning of each of these words. Then use each word in a sentence.

astronaut	**ghetto**
demonstration	**integration**

Skill Builder

Make a report about one of these famous Americans from the 1960s.

Maya Angelou	Ken Kesey
Rachel Carson	Martin Luther King
James Farmer	Malcolm X
Betty Friedan	Gloria Steinem
John Glenn	George Wallace

Chapter 28 Notes

Read over the chapter. Find answers to these questions:

1. What was the Peace Corps?
2. What was the Cuban missile crisis?
3. How did President Johnson and Congress help older Americans and the poor?
4. Why did some ghetto Blacks grow angry and hopeless during the 1960s?
5. What was the Black power movement?
6. Why did many Americans support the Vietnam War? Why did many Americans oppose it?

Be a Historian

Interview someone who remembers the assassination of President Kennedy, Senator Kennedy, or Martin Luther King. Ask that person these questions:

1. How did you feel when you heard about the assassination? How did other people react?
2. How do you think the assassination changed the country?

Bonus

Someone living in the 1960s would know the meanings of these words and phrases. Do you? Find out what each word or phrase means. Ask someone who remembers the 1960s.

Afro	generation gap	miniskirt
Beatlemania	hippie	peacenik
disco	mod	

Chapter 29 The Seventies and Eighties

NASA

Neil Armstrong, the first person to walk on the moon, took this picture of fellow astronaut Edwin Aldrin.

On July 20, 1969, two American astronauts landed on the moon. Americans had met the challenge President Kennedy set in 1961.

Since President Kennedy made that challenge, the world had changed rapidly. In 1961, the United States and the Soviet Union led the world in a cold war between communism and noncommunism.

In 1969, other countries had gained in strength. By then, Japan and the countries of western Europe had become economic leaders. Countries in the Middle East, Africa, Asia, and Latin America were making powerful alliances of their own.

By the 1980s, the United States would be working to develop friendly relations with communist countries.

- What was President Nixon's policy toward China and the Soviet Union?
- Why did Nixon resign as President?
- How did the United States and the Soviet Union try to control the arms race?
- How did President Reagan try to solve problems in the economy?

Key Words   You will be using these words in this chapter. Look them up in the glossary at the back of Part 2.

administration	**pardon**
hostage	**scandal**

Nixon's Plan to End the Vietnam War

During his campaign for President, Richard Nixon said he had a plan to bring about a "peace with honor." In 1969, President Nixon announced his plan. He called it the **Vietnamization** of the war.

Vietnamization meant turning over all the fighting of the war to South Vietnamese soldiers. Under the President's plan, the United States would train those troops, supply them with weapons, and support them with air power. But American combat troops would be gradually taken out of Vietnam and returned home.

The President's plan called for American planes to start bombing North Vietnam again. Nixon hoped to keep supplies from reaching the Vietcong in South Vietnam. He also hoped the bombing would force North Vietnam to seek peace.

American Forces Invade Cambodia

The North Vietnamese had military bases in Laos and Cambodia, two countries next to Vietnam. The President secretly ordered American troops to invade Cambodia.

Many Americans were angry when they learned that troops were in Cambodia. They accused the President of expanding the war. College students across America protested the invasion. Police and national guard troops were called in to keep order. At Kent State University in Ohio, troops shot and killed four students. At Jackson State University in Mississippi, two students were killed.

Looking Back
1. What did Vietnamization mean?
2. Why did some Americans protest the invasion of Cambodia?

Detente and an End to the War

President Nixon wanted to improve relations with the Soviet Union and China, the two communist "giants" of the world. He hoped their leaders could help persuade North Vietnam to end the Vietnam War. He also wanted to slow down the arms race, which he feared might lead to nuclear war.

In 1971, President Nixon began following a foreign policy called *detente* (day TAHNT). Its purpose was to relax tensions between noncommunist and communist countries.

Nixon Visits China

You read that the United States had refused to recognize Communist China since 1949. The United States acted as if that government did not exist. President Nixon ended that policy. In 1972, he visited Communist China. For the first time in over 20 years, the United States and China began to trade with each other.

Nixon Visits the Soviet Union

President Nixon also visited the Soviet Union in 1972. During that visit, President Nixon signed an agreement with **Leonid Brezhnev**, the Soviet leader. The treaty became known as **SALT I** (Strategic Arms Limitation Talks.) In it, the United States and the Soviet Union agreed to stop building certain kinds of nuclear weapons and to hold further talks. Brezhnev agreed also to talk to North Vietnamese leaders about ending the war.

A Vietnam Cease-Fire Is Signed

In January 1973, the United States, South Vietnam, North Vietnam, and the Vietcong signed a cease-fire agreement. In March, the last units of American troops left Vietnam.

Soon after American forces left, fighting broke out again in South Vietnam. In 1975, communist forces seized control of South Vietnam and united all Vietnam under one communist government.

U.S. Army Photograph #CC-33355

The Costs of the War

The Vietnam War was the longest war in America's history. More than 50,000 Americans died in Vietnam. More than 300,000 were wounded. The war had cost over 150 billion dollars.

The war left American soldiers bitter. Unlike veterans of other wars, Vietnam veterans were not welcomed home as heroes. And many veterans felt that they were forgotten by the government after the war.

The end of the war also left Americans divided. Some blamed the government for not doing more to save South Vietnam from communism. Others blamed the government for involving the nation in the war.

Many Americans could not understand how the United States had become part of the Vietnam War. The Constitution gives only Congress the power to declare war. But Congress had never declared war on North Vietnam. Presidents Johnson and Nixon had used their powers as commander in chief to send American troops to Vietnam.

In 1973, Congress passed the **War Powers Act**. The Act said that the President must tell Congress if he or she plans to send troops to fight overseas. The President also cannot send American forces into a conflict for more than 60 days without permission from Congress.

Looking Back

1. What was detente?
2. How did President Nixon improve relations with China and the Soviet Union?
3. What happened in Vietnam in 1975 after the war was over?

A CH-47A "Chinook" landed these U.S. troops in Vietnam in 1966.

The Watergate Scandal

In 1972, the Republican Party again nominated Richard Nixon as their candidate for President. In June of that year, five burglars were caught in the Democratic Party campaign headquarters in Washington, D.C. The headquarters were in a group of buildings named *Watergate*. The burglars had broken in to copy documents and wiretap the telephones.

Reporters Hint at a White House Scandal

News stories began to appear about a possible **scandal**. They said that people in the White House might have helped plan and pay for the burglary. The *FBI* (Federal Bureau of Investigation) began to investigate. It found evidence that two other people were connected with the burglary. One of them was a lawyer for the President's *campaign committee*. That was the group of Republicans who were planning Nixon's campaign for re-election.

President Nixon announced that the White House had also made an investigation. It showed no one in the White House had been involved in the break-in. In November, Nixon was re-elected as President.

A Cover-up Is Revealed

Early in 1973, the seven people connected with the burglary went on trial. All were found guilty and sentenced to prison terms. Then one of them revealed that witnesses had lied in court. He also said that certain White House officials had told the burglars to plead guilty so that the trial would end quickly. People began to suspect that the White House was trying to *cover up* the truth about the break-in. But President Nixon said he knew nothing about the break-in or a cover-up.

Congress Holds Investigation Hearings

Congress set up a special committee to investigate the break-in. Witnesses testified that important White House officials had ordered or approved the break-in. Then **John Dean** testified that he had helped cover up the facts about the break-in. He had been the *Presidential Counsel*, or President's lawyer. Dean also testified that the President had known about the cover-up and had ordered it to continue.

The committee also learned that the President had tape-recorded conversations he had held in his office. The committee asked for some of the tapes, but the President refused to give them up.

Vice-President Agnew Resigns

In 1973, another scandal troubled the Nixon **administration**. Government investigators charged Vice-President **Spiro Agnew** with filing false tax returns and accepting bribes. In October 1973, Agnew resigned. **Gerald Ford** became Vice-President.

President Nixon Resigns

The Supreme Court ruled that the President had to give up his tapes. The committee found that some tapes were missing. And part of one important tape had been erased. But enough remained to show that the President probably was part of a cover-up. A special House committee drew up *articles of impeachment*, or charges against the President. They charged that the President had *obstructed* justice (kept the courts from finding the truth), had misused his powers, and had kept evidence from Congress.

Before the House of Representatives could vote on impeachment, the President resigned. On August 9, 1974, Gerald Ford became the new President.

Looking Back
1. What was the Watergate scandal?
2. What impeachment charges did Congress make?

President Ford speaks to young Republicans in 1976. At his right is Mrs. Ford.

The Ford Years

After Nixon resigned, several people who had been part of his administration or 1972 campaign committee were put on trial. They were charged with perjury and obstructing justice. Most of them were sentenced to prison terms.

The Watergate scandal created a crisis in the United States government. But it showed the world that the Constitution, with its system of checks and balances, works: Congress and the Supreme Court had *checked* a President who seemed to break the law.

The scandal also showed that Americans believe in government based on ethics. *Ethics* are a strongly-held belief about what is right and what is wrong. Americans as a nation have always believed in truth, honesty, and high moral values: America will not accept government leaders or officials who break the law, who are dishonest, or who lie.

President Ford Pardons Nixon

President Ford wanted the nation to once again respect and trust its leaders. That would not happen, he believed, if a President were put on trial. In September 1974, the President *pardoned* Nixon. That meant Nixon could not be tried for crimes he might have committed as President.

Some Americans supported President Ford's decision. But other Americans did not. They felt that if Nixon had broken the law, he should stand trial.

America Has Inflation and Recession

When President Ford took office, the economy was suffering from severe *inflation*. During inflation, prices rise quickly. The dollar can't buy as many things as it had before. So, it is worth less.

To fight inflation, President Ford began a program he called **Whip Inflation Now (WIN)**. The President asked businesses not to raise prices. To help businesses keep prices down, he urged labor unions not to ask for large pay raises. High pay raises are one of the causes of high prices: When businesses raise their workers' wages, they must also raise prices to pay for the wages.

President Ford's WIN program was not successful. The government could not force businesses and unions to hold down prices and wages. Inflation continued to be a problem.

Then another problem developed: The economy began also to suffer a *recession*. During a recession, business slows down. People buy less; unemployment is high.

By 1974, the nation was in a period of both inflation and recession. And nearly 20 million Americans were without jobs.

Ford Loses to Jimmy Carter

In 1976, Republicans nominated Gerald Ford for President. Democrats nominated **Jimmy Carter**. Carter was the former governor of Georgia.

Many Americans blamed President Ford for the problems in the economy. Many also did not trust the President because he had pardoned Nixon.

Jimmy Carter became popular as a Washington "outsider." Carter had not served in the government in Washington, so many voters felt they could trust him. Carter defeated Ford in a close election.

Looking Back

1. Why did President Ford pardon Nixon?
2. What is inflation?
3. What is a recession?
4. Why did many Americans support Jimmy Carter for President?

The Carter Years

President Carter worked to establish peaceful relations between other countries and between the United States and the Soviet Union. But two world crises troubled his administration.

Carter Acts as Peacemaker

In 1978, President Carter invited the leaders of Egypt and Israel to the United States for peace talks. Egypt and Israel had been enemies since Israel became a nation in 1948.

The President met with the leaders. In September 1978, the three leaders signed an agreement called the **Framework for Peace in the Middle East**. In 1979, Egypt and Israel signed a peace treaty.

President Carter Signs a SALT Agreement

You read that the United States and the Soviet Union signed SALT I in 1972. In June 1979, President Carter signed a new agreement with the Soviet leaders. It became known as **SALT II**. It put more limits on the number of nuclear weapons the two countries could build. President Carter sent SALT II to the Senate for approval.

The Soviets Invade Afghanistan

In December 1979, Soviet forces invaded Afghanistan. Soviet leaders claimed they were helping the Afghanistan government put down a rebellion.

President Carter protested the invasion. He asked the Senate to put off any action on SALT II. (SALT II was never approved.) He also announced that American athletes would boycott the 1980 Olympic Games in Moscow. He stopped the sale of grain and banned the sale of high-technology equipment, such as computers, to the Soviet Union. He announced the United States would increase its military spending and that it would place new nuclear weapons in western Europe.

The Carter Doctrine Is Announced

The invasion of Afghanistan meant that Soviet forces were close to the Middle Eastern oil countries. President Carter was afraid that Soviet forces might move into those countries and cut off America and its allies from Middle Eastern oil.

The President pledged that America would come to the defense of any Middle Eastern country threatened by Soviet forces. That pledge became known as the **Carter Doctrine**.

A Crisis in the Middle East

Early in 1979, Moslem rebels in Iran overthrew the *shah*, the ruler of Iran. The United States had supported the shah's government for more than 20 years. The rebels' religious leader, **Ayatollah Khomeini**, became Iran's new ruler.

The shah fled to Mexico. Later in 1979, he came to the United States for medical treatment. Iran's new government demanded that the United States return the shah to Iran for trial. President Carter refused. Iranians seized the American embassy in Iran's capital city of Teheran. They took 63 Americans as *hostages*. They said they would free the hostages when the United States turned over the shah. Carter refused to meet their demands.

The hostage crisis continued throughout 1980. That year, Carter ran for re-election. His failure to free the hostages cost him votes in the election. He was defeated by **Ronald Reagan**. The hostages were set free on January 20, 1981—Carter's last day in office.

Looking Back
1. How did President Carter protest the Soviet invasion of Afghanistan?
2. What was the Carter Doctrine?
3. Why did Iranians take Americans hostage in 1979?

The Reagan Years

After the defeat in Vietnam, the Watergate scandal, and the Iran hostage crisis, Americans felt discouraged. President Reagan wanted people to feel good about their country and its future. ''We are too great a nation,'' he said, ''to limit ourselves to small dreams.''

Reagan Reduces the Size of Government

One of Ronald Reagan's goals as President was to reduce the size of the federal government. President Reagan believed the government had grown too large. He said that government interfered too much with business and in people's lives. It took too much away from people in taxes. It spent too much. And it made too many rules for business people to follow.

On his first day in office, President Reagan announced that he would cut over 30,000 jobs from the federal payroll. He also pledged to end many of the regulations that controlled business.

Reagan's Plan to Improve the Economy

President Reagan had a two-part plan to improve the economy: First, he called for a cut in taxes. The President argued that a tax cut would allow workers to keep more of their wages. Americans would then have more money to spend and invest. That would help the economy to grow.

Second, the President called for cuts in government spending. He believed heavy government spending led to inflation.

Congress went along with President Reagan's economic plan. It cut income taxes. It also approved Reagan's plan to cut spending on many *social programs*, or programs to help those in need, such as Medicare, Medicaid, and the food stamp program. (The food stamp program helps the needy buy food.)

At first, the economy went into a recession under Reagan's plan. But by 1984, the economy seemed to have recovered. Business was growing and inflation was under control.

The Budget Deficit Grows

The tax cut allowed many Americans to keep more of their wages. But the tax cut also meant that less money was coming into the national treasury. That helped to increase the nation's *budget deficit*. The deficit is a shortage of money to pay government expenses. A deficit exists when the government spends more money than it takes in through taxes.

Between 1981 and 1984, the President asked Congress for billions of dollars in increased defense spending. The President wanted to increase defense spending because he believed America had fallen behind the Soviet Union in the arms race.

Because of tax cuts and defense spending, the budget deficit nearly doubled under President Reagan.

The Election of 1984

Reagan ran for re-election in 1984. Several Democrats sought their party's nomination.

The Democrats nominated **Walter Mondale** of Minnesota to oppose Reagan. Mondale had served as Carter's Vice-President. Mondale chose **Geraldine Ferraro** to be his party's first woman candidate for Vice-President.

In his campaign, President Reagan appealed to American pride. ''America is back, standing tall,'' he told voters. Reagan won in 49 of the 50 states.

Looking Back
1. What was President Reagan's two-part plan to improve the economy?
2. Why did the budget deficit increase?

Outgoing President Carter briefs newly elected Ronald Reagan, at left.

President Reagan's Policies

During his second term, President Reagan countinued to talk with Soviet leaders about limiting nuclear weapons. He also continued to work to increase defense spending. In 1986, Congress agreed to spend over two billion dollars to develop a new anti-missile system.

America Aids Central America

President Reagan was especially concerned about two countries in Central America: Nicaragua and El Salvador.

For 42 years, Nicaragua had been ruled by a dictatorship. In 1979, a rebel army, the *Sandinistas*, overthrew the dictatorship.

President Reagan and many Americans feared that the Sandinistas had set up a communist government. They believed that the Sandinistas were sending military aid to communist rebels who were trying to overthrow the government in El Salvador.

President Reagan supported El Salvador in its fight against the rebels. He persuaded Congress to send American military advisors and millions of dollars in aid to El Salvador.

President Reagan also decided to send aid to Nicaraguan rebels fighting against the Sandinista government. The rebels were known as *Contras*. Reagan called the Contras "freedom fighters."

Many Americans disagreed with the President's decision. In 1984, Congress voted not to spend money to aid the Contras. But President Reagan convinced Congress in 1986 to send them aid.

Reagan Sends Troops to Trouble Spots

In 1982, Israeli troops attacked Palestinian guerrillas in Lebanon, a country in the Middle East. President Reagan sent U.S. Marines to Lebanon as part of UN peacekeeping forces.

In 1983, the prime minister of Grenada was killed. Grenada is an island nation in the Caribbean. Fighting broke out. President Reagan sent American troops to help a noncommunist government take control.

Reagan Protects American Interests

In the 1980s, Americans in Europe and the Middle East were being attacked by terrorists. Libya was known to be a training center for terrorists. It also supplied them with weapons. In 1986, an American soldier in Germany was killed in a nightclub that was bombed by terrorists. President Reagan ordered American planes to bomb Libya as punishment.

President Reagan also sent Americans to the Persian Gulf. The United States bought oil from Middle Eastern countries such as Kuwait. Tankers carrying the oil sailed through the Persian Gulf, past Iran and Iraq. Those two countries were at war with each other. They attacked ships in the Persian Gulf. The United States had sent American warships to protect the oil tankers. In 1987, President Reagan agreed to let some of the tankers sail under the American flag.

Looking Back

1. Why did President Reagan support the government in El Salvador, and the rebels (Contras) in Nicaragua?
2. Why were American warships sent to the Persian Gulf?

A special Congressional committee investigated the Iran-Contra affair. Daniel Inouye was chairman of the Senate committee.

The Iran-Contra Hearings

At the time of the Iran hostage crisis, the United States and Iran broke off official relations. All Americans left Iran.

Soon afterward, Iran and Iraq went to war. Iran wanted American weapons. United States policy was not to sell weapons to any country that supported terrorism and kidnapping of hostages. That included Iran.

President Reagan Sells Arms to Iran

In 1985, however, President Reagan secretly acted against that policy: He agreed to sell arms to Iran. Reagan had two reasons for his actions: He wanted to rebuild ties with Iran's leaders. And he wanted to free several American hostages being held in Lebanon. He believed Iran could free them.

Several planeloads of weapons were sent to Iran in 1985 and 1986. Three American hostages were set free in Lebanon. But three more were taken hostage.

In November 1986, Americans learned about the secret arms sale. Most Americans opposed it. They believed selling arms to try to "buy" hostages was a bad policy.

Money Goes to the Contras

Soon, Americans learned that three million dollars from the arms sale had been sent to the Contras in Nicaragua—at a time when Congress had cut off such aid. President Reagan said he had not known about that money being sent to the Contras. Many Americans did not believe him.

Congress set up a Joint Committee of the House and Senate to investigate the Iran-Contra affair. The Committee hearings began in May 1987 and went on through the summer. Many Americans followed the hearings on radio and television.

A Secret Foreign Policy

The Iran-Contra hearings revealed secret actions carried out by the **National Security Council (NSC)**. The NSC is a group of advisors to the President. NSC officials had taken part in both the arms sale to Iran and the transfer of money to the Contras. They had not told Congress about the arms sale. And they had not told the President about the transfer of money. During the hearings, NCS officials admitted that they had lied to Congress and destroyed documents.

Reactions to the Hearings

Many Americans were upset by what they learned during the hearings. Senator **Daniel Inouye** said there was no place in a democratic government for a "covert [secret] foreign policy...working outside the system...." Representative Lee Hamilton agreed. "Our government cannot function cloaked in secrecy," he said. "It cannot function unless officials tell the truth."

The Iran-Contra hearings reminded Americans that they live in a republic: Government leaders and officials must govern according to law. If they do not, they are violating the Constitution. Their actions will be stopped.

Looking Back

1. Why did President Reagan decide to sell arms to Iran?
2. What did National Security Council officials do with money from the arms sale?
3. Why were Americans upset by the Iran-Contra affair?

Chapter 29   Review

Facts First

Use words below to complete each sentence.

boycott   Middle East
Gerald Ford   Ronald Reagan
hostage crisis   taxes
inflation   Vietnamization
Iran-Contra hearings   Watergate scandal

1. President Nixon's plan to withdraw American troops from the Vietnam War was called _____.
2. The _____ caused President Nixon to resign.
3. _____ became President when President Nixon resigned.
4. The economy suffered from _____ during President Ford's administration.
5. President Carter called for a _____ of the Moscow Olympics.
6. The Iran _____ hurt President Carter's chances in the 1980 election.
7. _____ pledged to reduce the size of the federal government when he became President.
8. Reagan's economic plan called for cuts in _____ and government spending.
9. President Reagan sent troops to the Caribbean and the _____.
10. The _____ investigated foreign policy in Iran.

Word Check

Write the meaning of each of these words. Then use each word in a sentence.

administration   pardon
hostage   scandal

Skill Builder

Interview someone who remembers the Watergate hearings. Ask them:
1. How did you feel about the hearings?
2. Do you think Richard Nixon should have gone to trial? Why or why not?

Chapter 29 Notes

Read over the chapter. Find answers to these questions:
1. How did President Nixon end America's fighting in Vietnam?
2. How did United States policy toward China and the Soviet Union change under President Nixon?
3. What was the Watergate scandal?
4. What was the Carter Doctrine? Why did President Carter announce it?
5. What was the Iran hostage crisis?
6. What was President Reagan's two-part plan to improve the economy?
7. What were the Iran-Contra hearings?

Be a Historian

Events in Central America are still affecting the United States. Talk to someone who comes from Central America, or read newspapers and news magazines and listen to the news. Make a report about what is happening in Central America.

Bonus

Find out about one of these important women of the 1970s and 1980s. Then report what you learned:

Bella Abzug   Barbara Jordan
Shirley Chisholm   Coretta Scott King
Elizabeth Dole   Jeane Kirkpatrick
Geraldine Ferraro   Sandra Day O'Connor

Chapter 30   Challenges Today and Tomorrow

NASA astronauts show the effects of weightlessness on a slinky toy.

In 1787, delegates from the new United States met to write a new constitution. They created a flexible plan of government that could hold the nation together as it grew and changed.

The Constitution is now the oldest written plan of government being used in the world today. It has held the country together through more than 200 years of changes and challenges.

The United States is still a growing, changing nation. Americans will face many challenges in the years ahead. They may disagree over what actions to take. But Americans are united by the democratic ideals and ethics on which their nation was founded. And Americans will find ways to work together for the good of the nation—just as the delegates did more than 200 years ago.

- How have minority groups organized to improve America?
- How has the new immigration changed America?
- What new technology is changing how Americans live and work?
- What challenges do Americans face in the years ahead?

Key Words   You will be using these words in this chapter. Look them up in the glossary at the back of Part 2.

automation	**pollution**
cause	**tradition**

Americans Learn to Organize

The civil rights and Black power movements brought rights and opportunities to Blacks that they had not had before. Blacks also gained a new sense of pride in their abilities and in their history.

Other Americans also learned from those movements. They, too, began to take pride in their abilities and in their history. And they learned to organize themselves, as Blacks had, to work for their *causes*.

The Women's Movement

One of the largest movements organized in the 1960s was the **women's movement**.

All through America's history, working women held mostly low-paying jobs. Even when men and women held the same position, the women were paid less. Many women spoke out against such discrimination. In 1963, **Betty Friedan** told Americans about the problem in her book *The Feminine Mystique*.

In that same year, Congress passed the **Equal Pay Act**. That Act guaranteed that men and women doing the same work would receive the same pay. The Civil Rights Act of 1964 then prohibited job discrimination, including discrimination based on a person's sex.

Despite such laws, women still did not have equal rights. In 1966, Friedan and others set up the **National Organization for Women** (**NOW**). Together, they fought discrimination—in jobs, in education, and in the community.

The Equal Rights Amendment

Many Americans believed the only way to guarantee equal rights to women was to add an amendment to the Constitution. They urged Congress to pass the **Equal Rights Amendment** (**ERA**). That was an amendment that said, "Equality of rights under the law shall not be denied or abridged by the United States or any state on account of sex."

In 1972, Congress passed the ERA, and it went before the states to be ratified. At least 38 states had to ratify it, and they had to do it within ten years. Members of NOW and other Americans worked to get the amendment ratified. But some groups worked against it. They said that the ERA was not necessary, and that it would lead to harmful changes in American life.

By 1982, fewer than 38 states had ratified the ERA. It was defeated.

Even though the ERA was defeated, women continued to work for equal rights and opportunities. Women worked to open jobs and positions that were once only for men. More and more women have become doctors, lawyers, and scientists. In 1981, **Sandra Day O'Connor** became the first woman appointed to the U.S. Supreme Court. And, as you read, Geraldine Ferraro became the first woman nominated for Vice-President by a major party.

Disabled Americans Work for Change

In the 1960s, disabled Americans also began to organize in order to bring about change. At that time, many employers would not hire disabled Americans. By 1973, Congress had passed a law against such discrimination in many kinds of jobs.

Disabled Americans also worked to gain equal access to public buildings and transportation. City governments replaced some stairways and curbs with ramps for people using wheelchairs or walkers.

Jesse Jackson, *center*, campaigns in Los Angeles.

Elevators were equipped with numbers in Braille or sound systems that called out each floor to aid blind passengers. Parking spaces close to building entrances were set aside for the disabled. Trains and buses were designed for easier use by disabled passengers.

Older Americans Organize

Older Americans also learned to work for their cause. Many of them lived on social security payments. Those payments remained the same month after month. So, many older Americans faced poverty because of inflation: Prices were rising, but their incomes stayed the same.

Older Americans convinced the government to increase social security payments. They also called for improvements in medical care programs.

Older Americans fought against job discrimination as well. Many businesses forced people to retire when they reached age 65. Older Americans said it was unfair: Many workers were able and eager to keep working at that age. In 1978, Congress passed a law that said employers could not force workers to retire before age 70.

Looking Back

1. What laws helped to fight job discrimination against women?
2. How was the ERA defeated?
3. What changes has the women's movement brought about?
4. What changes have disabled Americans fought for?
5. What changes have older Americans brought about in social security payments and retirement age?

Minority Groups Organize

All across the country, groups of Americans in the 1960s and 1970s worked for more rights and opportunities. They began to work to end their problems.

Mexican Americans Help Their People

In the 1960s, Mexican Americans encouraged pride in *la raza*, or their culture. Some, such as **Jose Angel Gutierrez**, worked to elect people who would improve housing, education, and health care for Mexican Americans.

Cesar Chavez worked to help Mexican-American *migrant workers*. Those workers moved from farm to farm picking crops. They earned very low wages and often were provided with only shacks to live in. Chavez organized a union called the **United Farm Workers** (**UFW**). The UFW demanded that farmers raise wages and provide decent housing for farm workers. When farmers refused, UFW workers went on strike. They asked all Americans to boycott fruits and vegetables that came from non-union farms. Many Americans joined the boycott.

Native Americans Take Control

For many years, Native Americans were encouraged by the government to forget their culture—to give up their traditions for those of White Americans.

In the 1960s and 1970s, Native Americans worked to bring back their culture. They studied their history and brought back their *traditions*.

Native Americans also began to organize politically. Groups such as the **American Indian Movement** (**AIM**), founded by **Dennis Banks** and **Clyde Bellecourt**, held protests. They demanded an end to discrimination. They also demanded that Indians be given more control over their reservations. Many other Americans supported those protests.

These Native Americans march for their cause.

Asian Americans Become Political Leaders

Asian Americans also began to learn more about their history in America. Like other groups, they developed a new sense of pride. They, too, began to organize to work for change. They organized to get laws passed and leaders elected. For example, Daniel Inouye was a member of the 442nd Regiment of Japanese Americans in World War II. He was elected a member of the United States Senate in 1962.

Americans Form New Coalitions

By the 1980s, many minority groups in America had learned that, as organized groups, they held enough power to bring about change. And, they had also learned that they held even more power when their efforts had the support of others.

In the 1980s, minorities began to support each other as they worked toward goals they could share. For example, in 1984, civil rights leader **Jesse Jackson** campaigned for President. He called his supporters the "rainbow coalition." They were Americans of all colors. Jackson promised to work for changes that would benefit *all* Americans, including minorities.

Looking Back
1. How did Mexican Americans bring about change in their situation?
2. What changes did Native Americans work for?
3. How did minorities help each other in the 1980s?

The New Immigrants

In the 1920s, Congress put limits on immigration. Fewer Europeans were allowed into this country. No immigration was allowed from Asia.

Then, in 1965, Congress passed a new immigration law. It opened America again to immigrants from all parts of the world.

Changing Immigration Patterns

After 1965, immigrants began arriving from Cuba, the Dominican Republic, Jamaica, and other Caribbean countries. Immigrants also began coming from Korea, China, and the Philippines. Many of those new immigrants had fled to the United States as *political refugees*. They had left their home countries because they were not safe from the governments in power.

Thousands of political refugees from Vietnam, Cambodia, and Laos began arriving in the 1970s. As you read in Chapter 29, United States troops left Vietnam in 1973. In 1975, the Vietnam War ended, and the communist government of of North Vietnam took control of South Vietnam. The governments of Cambodia and Laos also fell to communists. The new government of Cambodia was especially cruel to its people: Between one and three million Cambodians died after the takeover.

Adapting to a New Home in America

Many refugees who came to the United States could not speak English. Those who came from small rural or mountain villages were bewildered by life in America. Special programs were set up by state and federal governments, and by community, religious, and other private organizations. Those programs helped the new immigrants learn to live in America and to become Americans. The programs taught newcomers English and job skills. The programs also taught citizenship.

These Mein (pronounced mee-in) women have immigrated from Laos. They are learning the American money system. They will share their culture with other Americans.

Contributions of the New Immigrants

The new immigrants settled all over the United States. Like other immigrant groups in America's history, many new immigrants settled together in certain neighborhoods in towns and cities. They brought their traditions and customs with them to those neighborhoods. Many opened their own businesses, such as stores and ethnic restaurants.

The new groups of immigrants are helping to shape America, just as every immigrant group has done. Immigrants bring with them the customs, religions, languages, art, literature, music, and foods of many lands. They add to the culture of America. For example, foods such as *pizzas*, *tacos*, *eggrolls*, and *yogurts* are eaten by Americans today. All were first brought to America by immigrants.

Each new wave of immigrants, from the first Americans to the earliest European settlers to the most recent arrivals, has helped make America what it is today.

Looking Back

1. Why have many new immigrants come to America?
2. How have government and private programs helped immigrants adapt to life in America?
3. How have immigrants added to American culture?

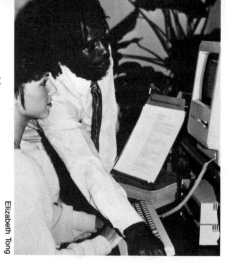

These office workers use a computer to keep track of business records and accounts.

The Age of Technology

Since World War II, technology and new inventions have greatly changed American life. Technology has brought such great change that historians sometimes call the years since the war the "Age of Technology."

Technology Allows People to Live Longer

Today, Americans live longer and healthier lives because of new medical technology. Researchers have developed vaccines to prevent diseases such as smallpox and polio. Doctors can now replace many diseased organs of the human body with *transplants* (organs removed from other people). Often, the patients receiving those transplants can then live normal lives.

In 1900, the average person in America lived to the age of 47. By 1984, the average American lived to age 74.

Technology in Space

Advances in technology also allowed the United States to make great progress in space exploration in the 1970s and 1980s. American astronauts first landed on the moon in 1969. By 1972, American spacecraft had carried astronauts to the moon six different times.

In the late 1970s, American scientists and engineers developed the first *space shuttle*. (A space shuttle carries people and cargo into space. Then it returns to Earth to be launched again.)

Unmanned spacecraft were also launched into space in the 1970s and 1980s. Some were communications satellites that allowed radio and television signals to be broadcast around the world. Others explored distant planets and sent back information. In 1976, the spacecraft *Viking I* landed on Mars. *Voyager II* is expected to pass Neptune in 1989, and send back pictures of that planet.

Technology Changes the Workplace

Technology has changed the way Americans work. During the 1950s, advances in technology led to the growth of **automation**. More and more, machines were used to do work once done by people.

One of the most useful new machines was the *computer*. The first computers were large and expensive, but, during the 1960s, engineers developed smaller and less expensive computers. By the 1980s, most businesses were using them.

Computers have changed the way offices and factories are run. Offices use computers to send out customers' bills, keep track of expenses, and do other work once done by office workers. In some factories, computer-run *robots* work on assembly lines. (A robot is a machine that can do the work a person does.)

Computers, robots, and other machines have taken jobs away from people. But the machines have also created many new jobs: Skilled workers are needed to produce, run, and maintain the machines. In the 1980s, technical training became more and more important.

Looking Back

1. How has technology helped Americans live longer and healthier lives?
2. What have communications satellites done for people on Earth?
3. How has automation changed the way people work?

Challenges Ahead

Americans today face many challenges. And the future will bring more. These pictures show four such challenges. How do you think Americans can meet them?

Social Programs to Aid Americans   In 1986, former President Jimmy Carter joined "Habitat for Humanity" in building housing for low-income families. Millions of Americans need help such as housing, food, and health programs. The United States must find a way to balance its budget and still provide funds for social programs. The efforts of private citizens such as those in this picture can help. They can help make life better for all Americans.

Pollution Control to Save Our Planet   This barge filled with garbage has no place to go. In June 1987, the garbage was turned away at dump sites that were already full. America and other nations continue to dump wastes into the air, land, and water of our planet. Such pollution damages the atmosphere, rain forests, and oceans that are necessary for life on Earth. People everywhere need to be aware of the dangers of pollution and find ways to control it.

New Sources of Safe Energy   The United States uses tremendous amounts of energy. Some of it comes from oil, which America imports from Middle Eastern countries. When trouble breaks out in those countries, America's oil supply is threatened. Burning oil causes another problem for America. It pollutes the environment.

Americans have begun using new sources of energy. But those new sources also cause problems. For example, this electric power plant uses nuclear fuel. In 1979, an accident happened at the plant. The accident could have caused radioactive contamination in the surrounding area. Americans continue to face the challenge of finding safe ways to provide America with inexpensive, "clean" energy.

Cooperation among Nations   In April 1987, leaders of the United States and the Soviet Union met to discuss nuclear arms control and international relations. Nuclear weapons could destroy the world. And starvation and military conflicts threaten to destroy millions of people daily. America must continue to work for arms control and cooperation among nations. Such cooperation is needed to feed the world's people. And such cooperation is needed to end conflicts and the nuclear threat to the world.

Chapter 30

Review

Facts First

Choose the *two* endings that can complete each sentence.

1. The women's movement fought to
   a. defeat the Equal Rights Amendment.
   b. end discrimination against women.
   c. open to women jobs that were once for men only.

2. Minority groups in the 1960s and 1970s
   a. worked against discrimination.
   b. organized to get leaders elected to office.
   c. had no problems finding jobs and housing.

3. After 1965, large numbers of immigrants came to America
   a. from Caribbean countries.
   b. as political refugees.
   c. from the Soviet Union.

4. Government and private programs
   a. provide English classes for immigrants.
   b. do nothing to aid immigrants.
   c. teach immigrants citizenship.

5. New technology has
   a. helped Americans to live longer.
   b. changed the way many Americans work.
   c. ended America's space program.

6. Computers and other machines
   a. help office work get done faster.
   b. do not need people to run or maintain them.
   c. have made technical training important for people seeking work.

Word Check

Write the meaning of each of these words. Then use each word in a sentence.

automation   pollution
cause   tradition

Skill Builder

Some of these people immigrated to the United States. Others are the children or grandchildren of immigrants. Find out about one of these people. Then report what you learned.

Issac Asimov   Patrick Ewing
Mikhail Baryshnikov   John Kenneth Galbraith
Zbigniew Brzezinski   Henry Kissinger
Henry Cisneros   Ted Koppel
Mario Cuomo   Madeleine May Kunin

Chapter 30 Notes

Read over the chapter. Find answers to these questions:

1. Why did some people support the ERA? Why did some people oppose it?
2. How did Mexican Americans and Native Americans work to bring about change?
3. Why have the new immigrants come to America? Where have they come from?
4. How do immigrants contribute to America?
5. How has automation changed the way Americans work?

Be a Historian

Find out about a problem Americans face today, such as crime, drugs, or health threats. Then write a report about it.

Bonus

Choose a problem facing Americans today. Set up a debate in your class to discuss a possible solution to that problem.

Unit 10

Review

What Do You Know?

Use words below to complete each sentence.

defense	organize	refugees
energy	Peace Corps	resigned
invasion	poverty	Technology
	protests	

1. President Kennedy set up the _____ to help people in poor nations.
2. President Lyndon Johnson declared a war on _____.
3. There were _____ in America because people disagreed about the Vietnam War.
4. President Richard Nixon _____ after the Watergate scandal was investigated.
5. President Jimmy Carter protested against the Soviet _____ of Afghanistan.
6. President Ronald Reagan asked Congress to increase _____ spending.
7. Women and minority groups learned to _____ to bring about changes.
8. Many immigrants came to America as political _____ after 1965.
9. Computers are part of the "Age of _____."
10. Americans are working to find new sources of _____ for the United States.

What Do You Think?

Some people believe that crime, poverty, and disease are increasing in the nation. Many believe a nuclear war with the Soviet Union cannot be avoided.

Other people believe Americans can overcome their problems and avoid nuclear war.

What do you believe? Why?

Skill Builder

Find out in what years these events happened. Then write them in order.
- The last American troops leave Vietnam.
- President Kennedy is assassinated.
- Democrats nominate Geraldine Ferraro for Vice-President.
- Martin Luther King is assassinated.
- Iranians seize American hostages.
- Americans land on the moon.

Unit 10 Notes

Look over the unit to find answers to these questions:

1. How did President Johnson and Congress fight a "war on poverty"?
2. How did the Vietnam War divide Americans?
3. What problem developed between the United States and the Soviet Union under
   a. President Kennedy?
   b. President Carter?
4. How did the United States become involved in Nicaragua and El Salvador?
5. How has technology changed the lives of Americans?
6. What are some challenges facing Americans in the years ahead?

Word Builder

Write a story about American life the way you would like it to be in the future. Use all the key words listed below.

Key Words

automation	inflation
cause	integration
demonstration	pollution
ghetto	recession

Glossary Part 2

ad min is tra tion the people and departments that make up the executive branch of government, under the control of the President; a President's term of office

ag gres sion an attack made by one nation against another

ap peal to ask that a court case be heard again by a higher, more powerful court

arms race the competition among nations to build the most powerful weapons

as sem ble to build something by putting it together piece by piece

as tro naut a member of the United States space program who is trained to travel in space

au to ma tion the use of machines to do jobs once done by people

black list to refuse to hire someone because that person is suspected of disloyalty

boom a time of rapid growth, especially for a business or an industry

cap i tal ism an economic system under which individuals, rather than the government, own and control the nation's property and businesses; the economic system of the United States

cause a movement based on certain strong beliefs of its followers *Many people supported the migrant workers' cause in 1965.*

co lo ni al ism the rule of one nation over other lands and peoples

com mu nism an economic system under which property and businesses are owned by a whole nation instead of by individuals; the economic system that the Soviet Union is based on

com pe ti tion the efforts of businesses to attract more customers and sell more goods than other businesses

con sum er a person who buys goods, such as food, clothing, and appliances

dem on stra tion an event, such as a march or rally, meant to protest or show support of something

dic ta tor a ruler who has total control over a country

dis crim i nate to treat certain people differently (unfairly) because of their race, sex, age, etc.

draft a system for signing people up to serve in the armed forces

eth nic describing a group of people of the same race or national background

fi nan ces the ways in which a government collects and spends money

ghet to a city neighborhood, usually poor and rundown, where one kind of minority group lives

hear ing an investigation made by Congress, during which witnesses are called to answer questions

home stead er a person who is given government land in return for the promise to live on and farm it

hos tage a person held prisoner until some demand is met

hu man rights rights that should belong to all people everywhere

in dus try all the businesses that produce a certain kind of goods, such as food or automobiles

in te gra tion the mixing together of people of different races, nationalities, etc.

in va sion entering an area in large numbers *An invasion of gold seekers filled the Black Hills;* an attack on a nation or area in order to take control *In World War II, thousands of Allied soldiers took part in the D-Day invasion of France.*

i so late to keep a nation apart from others—out of their affairs or problems

isth mus a narrow strip of land that connects two large land areas

la bor u nion a group of workers who organize in order to bargain for higher wages and better working conditions

man u fac ture to make or produce goods to be sold by a business

mar kets places where a nation can sell its goods *American farmers sold much of their food to foreign **markets** during World War II.*

min i mum wage the lowest amount per hour that an employer can legally pay to a worker *Congress sets the **minimum wage** in the United States.*

neu tral taking no sides in a conflict

par don to forgive or release from punishment

pol i cy a plan of the government to deal with important matters, such as foreign trade, taxes, etc.

pol lu tion the release of harmful material into air, land, or water

prod uct the kind of goods made by a business to sell

pro duc tiv i ty the amount of goods that factories produce in a day

pros per i ty a time when business is good and most people have jobs and money to spend

ra tion to allow people to buy only a limited amount of certain kinds of goods

ref u gee a person who flees to a foreign country to find safety from danger, such as persecution or warfare

reg u la tion control through rules and laws

re la tions dealings between nations

scan dal a situation or actions that shock people's sense of right and wrong

seg re gate to keep one group apart from others, usually unfairly *Many schools were **segregated** in the South.*

stock mar ket the place where people buy and sell stock

strike refusing to work because of a disagreement with an employer about wages or working conditions

sub urb a community, including homes, schools, and businesses, built near a city

sum mit con fer ence a special meeting of world leaders

tech nol o gy the ways that people use scientific knowledge, inventions, and discoveries

to tal i tar i an having total control over a nation and the lives of its people *Lenin set up a **totalitarian** government in the Soviet Union.*

tra di tion a belief or custom passed from one generation to the next, and so on

trans con ti nen tal across a continent

un em ploy ment being without a job

wel fare help that the government gives people to improve their well-being, such as social security pensions and food stamps

world af fairs events that happen in various parts of the world, involving more than one nation

zone a section of land marked off as separate from the surrounding area for a certain reason

Index Part 2

Italicized page numbers refer to illustrations. The *m* or *p* before each number refers to a *m*ap or *p*icture on the page.

Congratulations!

You are an informed American. You now know about the history of your country. You learned what happened to the country in its second hundred years:

• how American technology helped the country to grow and become strong;

• how the United States became a world power and the leader of democratic nations;

• how the Constitution keeps the United States government working through crises and change;

• how Americans continue to work to bring equal rights and freedoms to all Americans; and

• how immigrants continue to shape America and make it strong.